To the Honour of
Jerry McCabe

To the Honour of Jerry McCabe

Dermot Walsh
with
Ann McCabe

BLACKWATER PRESS

Editor
Adam Brophy

Design & Layout
Paula Byrne

Cover Design
Karen Hoey

ISBN 1-84131-906-6
EAN 978-1-84131-906-3

Produced in Ireland by
Blackwater Press
c/o Folens Publishers
Hibernian Industrial Estate
Tallaght
Dublin 24

Acknowledgements

While the authorisation and support of Ann McCabe and her brother-in-law, Pat Kearney, were essential, this book would not have been possible without Diarmaid Mac Dermott of Ireland International News Agency, and the archives and library of *The Irish Examiner*.

The very major problem of sourcing court records was solved by Diarmaid Mac Dermott whose work included coverage of five trials for the capital murders of Gardaí at the Special Criminal Court. His records from the McCabe trial and from other trials were of inestimable value.

Exceptional also was the co-operation and support from *The Irish Examiner*. Through the good offices of deputy editor Brian Carroll, a Limerick man who attended school with members of the McCabe family, and Ann Kearney of the editorial management team, full access was opened up to the excellent archives and library. The very highest gratitude is owed to Paul McCarthy for exhaustive searching and checking of records, and for unfailing assistance and guidance. Special thanks also to Pat Moloney and the other members of the library staff at the paper.

Grateful acknowledgement is due to *The Limerick Leader* archives at Limerick City Library and for the assistance provided by staff of the National Library, the Clare County Library and other county library staff who assisted in the search through newspaper records.

My thanks to Liam Burke of Press 22 and Kieran Clancy of *The Examiner* picture agency for permission to reproduce the cover shots of Ann and Jerry McCabe.

The Adare commemorative plaque outside Adare Garda Station, pictured on the back cover, is by Limerick artist Una Heaton who designed the memorial on commission from Limerick County Council.

In cross-checking events and dates, this book has also drawn on the superb *Lost Lives* chronicles of all those who died during the Northern Ireland conflict from 1970 by David McKittrick, Seamus Kelters, Brian Feeney and Chris Thornton; *A Secret History of the IRA* by Ed Moloney; *Armed Struggle – A History of the IRA* by Richard English; and *The Informer* by Sean O'Callaghan.

Most special thanks to those who shared confidential information with me and who cannot be acknowledged by name. Their assistance is greatly appreciated and it is hoped that their trust has been vindicated by this book.

Dermot Walsh
November 2006

Dedication

This book is dedicated to the memory of the parents of Jerry McCabe, the late Johnny and Lizzie McCabe, and to the other members of the family who shared in the agony and anguish of Ann McCabe:

Michael and Katy McCabe
Marie and Liam O'Leary
Eileen and Pat Kearney
Nuala and Cameron Heaton
Kay and Eamon Conway

Contents

Foreword

This book sets out the reasons and background to why I stood up to confront Mr Gerry Adams, President of Sinn Féin, in a bar in the Bronx, New York, during St Patrick's Day celebrations in 2006.

I was standing up in the cause of justice for my husband, the detective Garda gunned down in cold blood in Adare on the day that the world changed for me and my family. It was almost ten years since the full-of-life presence of Jerry McCabe had been snatched away from me, his wife, and his extended family. In all that time my questions had been unanswered. They remained unanswered in the Bronx.

Before that terrible June Friday in Adare, it would have been unthinkable for Ann McCabe to stand up and address any gathering. I was a housewife, a hairdresser, a mother and a grandmother. The thought of speaking before the President of Ireland or groups that included leaders and statesmen, diplomats and public figures of international repute would have been a panic-inducing nightmare.

In the cause of truth and justice I have carried a torch for Jerry McCabe in my efforts to penetrate double standards and double talk, and cast light onto the shadowy, subversive world and ambivalent language of political expediency.

It has not been easy. But I have not been alone. Unswerving support and encouragement has been unfailing from our children, my mother, Jerry's late father, his brothers and sisters, as well as the varying Garda bodies and loyal and steadfast friends including a great number who were remote figures or strangers before June 1996. Right through the decade there has been a constant flow of messages of sympathy, solidarity and support from every level of society in Ireland and abroad. They ranged from the rural pensioner who walked miles to her Garda station to hand in a Mass card, to leaders in political and civic life in the USA, the UK, Northern Ireland and the country my husband served. I count them as people who understand the nature of my loss, and my desire to move on and attempt to make the future better than the past through affirming those who promote, preserve and protect the rule of law.

Yet there were desolate times when I felt very much on my own.

Back at the close of 2004 when I heard that the release of the killers of my husband was 'on the table', it seemed that I was one of the only people to question this act. I wondered how a better future could be ushered in on the back of such an obvious injustice? How could the rule of law be debased in this way? However, the consensus seemed to be that this was the price that 'we' had to pay for the 'peace process', and that to take any other course was to oppose this process.

I have been categoric in my support for the peace process. Why would I think otherwise, as I have seen at first hand what happens when violence becomes the norm in politics? On many occasions I have reminded my listeners that one of the most abiding memories people have of the news reports from Adare on the day of the shooting was that the media cameras picked out the sticker on the rear of the Garda escort car. The small white rectangle read, 'I'm for PEACE'.

One of the trademarks of republican mythology is the list of patriots who 'died for Ireland'. My husband died for Ireland. It was not his choice and it was not mine. But Jerry died to protect our peaceful society and this peace must be defended by all right-thinking people. The Ireland my husband died for is a place where marches of all kinds can be held, and where different shades of opinion can debate their views with words as opposed to bricks, stones and bullets. Jerry McCabe's Ireland is the country where politics is conducted through persuasion and argument and where the term 'republican' once again comes to stand for a political ethos where Church, State and legislature are separate, where the rights and responsibilities of the individual are respected and dissenting voices are accorded freedom of expression. In the country that Jerry McCabe died for, posing questions does not mean being anti-peace.

When, with all and sundry forecasting the imminent release of the murder gang, I publicly asked whether Bertie Ahern or the IRA ran the country, I felt very alone. So, it was with a great sense of pride, mingled with relief, that I saw the people of Ireland begin to voice their disquiet at the turn of events. Since then, such doubts have been proven to be correct. It has become clear that a person can be 'for' the peace process without losing the capacity to think intelligently or to ask questions of Sinn Féin.

While one of the saddest aspects of recent times was the murder of Robert McCartney, one of the most heartening was the sight and sound of his five sisters and his partner demanding answers and refusing to become complicit in the Provisional IRA's enforced code of silence.

Those brave women – the sisters, Claire, Catherine, Paula, Gemma, Donna and the murdered Robert's partner, Bridgeen – focused the minds of the Irish people and of powerful Irish-American interests on the horrors of power without responsibility. Their stance also raised the spectre of intimidation of witnesses which emerged so clearly around the trial of the Adare killers.

It is the positive and peace-building legacy of Jerry McCabe that provided me and many allies and friends with the platform to continue to pose questions.

On the weekend that changed our lives, the then US Ambassador to Ireland joined our grieving family in Limerick to change our lives in a forward-looking and future-shaping way. Ms Jean Kennedy Smith, who has become a dear and exceptionally treasured friend, took immediate steps to commemorate Jerry McCabe on both sides of the Atlantic. Working with the head of the US Immigration Pre-Inspection service at Shannon Airport, an exchange programme was established between the Garda force and the John Jay College of Criminal Justice police training academy in New York. The Jerry McCabe Fellowship Awards which I announce each St Patrick's week in New York have been most generously supported by subscribers committed to the principles of justice and law enforcement. It is a matter of great pride that our first child, John, who was a serving member of the Garda force when his father was gunned down, was the first recipient of the bursary awarded in the name of the murdered guardian of the peace, who died to guard that very peace.

Other bridges of understanding and trust have been built in the name of Jerry McCabe. Through the low-key work of the Irish Peace Institute at the University of Limerick, bonds have been established with the widows of police officers in Northern Ireland and also with the organisation that unites all survivors of police officers in the UK and Northern Ireland. Drawing on the expertise and experience of those organisations, I have had the privilege of joining with the Garda Representative Association in the formation of the Garda Survivors' Support Association. With the immediate past President of the GRA, Dermot O'Donnell, as its founder patron, I was most honoured to accept the invitation to serve as its founding president.

The memory of Jerry McCabe has also been honoured with two memorials in Adare, by a bust at Henry Street Garda headquarters carved by Limerick sculptor Jim Connolly, and with a civics award at his Rockwell College alma mater. His name has also been enshrined by medals and awards on both sides of the Atlantic. However, my family and I will never be in need of a memorial of any kind. Jerry McCabe is the first thought in our minds each waking morning, and the last in our thoughts each night. My own life, the memories of our happiness, the faces of our children and grandchildren, always remind me of Jerry. Their lives and my own are living memorials to the man that he was.

The spirit of Jerry McCabe lives. Just as his memory and the brutal nature of his killing have become embedded in the public consciousness, questions will also endure. It was to present those questions in an ordered manner that I consented to authorise and support this book by Dermot Walsh.

I stood up for Jerry McCabe's truth and justice in New York when I faced the Sinn Féin President, Mr Gerry Adams, among his Irish-American supporters. I asked who had given the authorisation to shoot down my detective husband in cold blood in Adare.

My question was not answered by Mr Adams.

But the questions have not gone away.

Ann McCabe
October 2006

Chapter 1

The village of Adare is a monument to peace and understanding. More of a storybook than a picture postcard village, the welcoming openness of its unusually wide village streets and the captivating visual appeal of its layout is the legacy of local pride shared between the old and the new, the titled landlord and the native people.

The calm charm of Adare reflects centuries of harmony and partnership. While establishing what was acknowledged in the nineteenth century as one of the finest baronial residences in all Ireland, the Earls of Dunraven also devoted time and money to development of the village that fringed the estate Thady Quin had purchased from the great Geraldine Gaelic Lords of Munster.

In a tasteful replacement of the old and dilapidated, the second Earl of Dunraven built the Tudor-style houses and also endowed the village with facilities for visitors, traders and locals. The landlord built a quay for vessels using canal access to the village. Other developments promoted by the landlord included a hotel, a fever hospital and a dispensary. The Earl of Dunraven also provided Adare with a post office. A later successor to the title, the fourth Earl of Dunraven, would site a village hall landmark at the head of the broad street and build two rows of cottages in 1911.

The proud centrepiece of the village is Adare Manor. At the heart of an estate surrounded by ancient abbeys dating back to the early thirteenth century, with meadows freshened by the river Maigue, a deer park extending over 400 acres and a thick crown of forestry, the manor was a labour of love by the second Earl of Dunraven and his wife, Caroline.

Retaining only some of the walls from the mansion dating from his great-grandfather's time, the second Earl of Dunraven spared nothing in building a manor of great style and character.

With its 365 windows and 52 chimney pots as conversation pieces, and surrounded by the symmetry of boxed gardens, the Lord and Lady of the manor brought in the best of celebrated professionals and artfully skilled locals to realise the dream residence.

Local stone and timber carvers drawn from Adare and the surrounding countryside, as well as local workmen, were employed alongside the pioneer of Gothic revival design, architect Augustus Welby Northmore Pugin, during the 21 years of building.

Pugin, whose signature features in the style of many churches in Ireland, designed the carved grey stone chimney piece in the great hall, several other marble chimney pieces, the paneled walls and ceilings of the dining room and the minstrels' gallery. He also designed the elegant staircase of carved oak.

It was on that staircase that two familiar faces caught the eye of Desmond O'Malley at the end of April 1996.

From his election in 1968 to Dáil Éireann, after a bitter east Limerick by-election that involved the widow of his uncle who he eventually succeeded, Desmond O'Malley was never far from power, controversy and danger. He had hardly warmed his parliamentary seat when he was promoted by then Taoiseach, Jack Lynch, to the second layer sub-cabinet rank of Parliamentary Secretary. In the sensational political upheaval of the 1970 arms' crisis when two senior and exceptionally prominent ministers were dismissed amid allegations of gun-running to the beleaguered people of the North, Des O'Malley was cast into high profile and high risk as Minister for Justice. He came to that office at a fevered period when the simmering northern unrest of the 1960s had blazed into armed warfare. An outspoken and resolute opponent of subversion, as Minister he introduced the Special Criminal Court.

He remained a fierce critic of subversive elements, criminality and political corruption when taking a public stand against Charles Haughey's leadership of the Fianna Fáil party. His adamant refusal to come to heel led to his expulsion from Fianna Fáil and his formation of the Progressive Democrats party which would become a pivotal influence in Irish politics from the second half of the 1980s.

Even though he occupied the opposition bench in 1996, decades of outstanding service in a variety of ministries and a record that was second to none as an advocate who delivered for his city, county and region made Desmond O'Malley one of the most recognised and respected figures in Irish politics when he stepped into Adare Manor on Monday, 29 April 1996.

O'Malley was in distinguished company, and not only from Ireland. Luminaries and household names from the world of parliamentary politics in the Republic, Northern Ireland and Britain had gathered in Adare for a plenary session of the British-Irish Inter-Parliamentary Body. Formally established six years earlier to build bridges of understanding on the common ground shared by parliamentarians of Ireland and Britain, the body stemmed from a 1980 summit meeting between the Irish Taoiseach, Charles Haughey, and the British Prime Minister, Margaret Thatcher.

The parliamentary body met in plenary session twice a year with the venues alternating between the two jurisdictions. It was another outstanding champion of Limerick, lifetime socialist campaigner Jim Kemmy, then representing the Labour Party, who was instrumental in bringing the three-day plenary session and focus of international political and media attention to Adare and the manor which had become a luxury hotel under American ownership in the 1980s.

Des O'Malley was mingling with his fellow members of the parliamentary body at a pre-dinner reception in the lofty ornate splendour of Adare Manor when he looked up to see a couple of faces that he knew exceptionally well.

In his years as a minister, and particularly in his 1970s term of office as Minister for Justice, the intensive security operation surrounding O'Malley included Limerick plain clothes detective members of the Special Branch, Jerry McCabe and Ben O'Sullivan. They had been promoted to the Special Branch at the same time and, from the day they teamed up, had become virtually inseparable friends.

For the two detectives, the Adare security duty for the British-Irish parliamentary body was almost a get-together or reunion with leading political figures from Britain as well as Ireland that they had guarded over the years.

Besides former Minister O'Malley, the 25 members of the British-Irish body drawn from both the Dáil and the Westminster parliaments included former ministers and others who had visited Limerick in the past and come under the protection of the Special

Branch. Among them were Michael O'Kennedy of Fianna Fáil and Peter Barry of Fine Gael, both of whom had held the Minister for Foreign Affairs portfolio as well as other ministerial office. Others in attendance from the Dáil included former Minister for Health, Dr Rory O'Hanlon, and his Fianna Fáil party colleagues, Dermot Ahern and John O'Donoghue, who had both served as Ministers of State. Also present from the Labour ranks was Seamus Pattison who had also been a Minister of State.

From the British parliament, the attendance included former holders of the Secretary of State for Northern Ireland office, Lord Merlyn Rees of Labour and Tom King of the Conservative party as well as Stanley Orme who had served in the Northern Ireland office. Other household names present were deputy leader of the SDLP in Northern Ireland, Seamus Mallon, and Peter Temple-Morris, a leading Conservative backbench authority on Northern Ireland affairs who was co-chairman of the inter-parliamentary body that year with Paul Bradford of Fine Gael.

Des O'Malley slipped away from his fellow parliamentarians when he spotted his old minders looking down on him from the vantage point of the great carved oak staircase.

They were pleased to see and greet each other. The two Garda officers had moved up to Special Branch detective rank in 1972 just when O'Malley was finishing his term as an exceptionally youthful Minister for Justice. They had joined the other 'Branch men' when the minister had thrown a party for them as an expression of appreciation for their round-the-clock vigilance on his home and movements.

As he ascended the stairs to where the two detectives were seated on the upper steps, O'Malley could not help noticing that what appeared to be a young woman of hardly more than schoolgoing age was sitting directly below the two detectives. She was dressed casually in jeans, and on her lap was an Uzi sub-machine gun. As he reached the detectives, he observed that things had changed a great deal in the Garda force as he nodded to the young woman member of the Special Branch.

Even before he spotted his former security guards, the former Minister for Justice had been intrigued by the exceptional level of security on show in Adare.

After an exchange of greetings, he remarked on the large number of security personnel in evidence around the manor, its estate and the village of Adare.

'Why so many?' he asked, and especially why so many in Adare of all places. He wondered aloud if there was any danger or threat.

'Oh, Adare is grand,' replied Detective Jerry McCabe. 'There is no danger in Adare. But there could be from places quite close by.'

39 days later Detective Garda Jerry McCabe lay dead beside his wounded colleague in their unmarked Garda car. They had been on security escort duty with a post office delivery truck. Jerry McCabe was killed instantly in a burst of gunfire. He lay dead in the quiet rising hours on the morning of Friday, 7 June 1996. He lay dead in Adare.

Chapter 2

The earthy intimacy of their parting banter constituted a statement in itself. After 27 years of marriage and five children, the abiding physical attraction and mutual mature passion of Ann and Jerry McCabe still sparked in their marriage. The proof was in the coded communication of the closest of partnerships that only comes with time and the almost telepathic understanding that underpins a shared sense of humour. They were, in the words that their first son would put on public record, 'a couple in love and united'.

Jerry was on the early shift that made up one third of his six-day roster. It was early morning and he was the only one up in the family home at Avondale Drive, in the comfortable suburb of Greystones. The estate was wedged between Limerick's twin sporting pillars of the Gaelic Grounds and Thomond Park. Today, he was on security escort duty with cash in transit movement by post office truck to a string of calls outside the city that would take him towards the county border with his native Kerry. His birthplace, Ballylongford, sat on the banks of the Shannon just a few miles into the footballing supreme Kingdom county.

Like any family home, the father's workday routines were part of the sounds that heralded a new morning and, like any wife, Ann McCabe was drowsily aware of her husband's movements. He was starting work at an hour when most of the country would still be asleep. He was going to be sitting in an unmarked patrol car for the duration of his working day. But he was looking for a fresh shirt. A shirt that had been ironed. That was her Jerry.

The shirt was located and he was on his way. The quiet words that she would remember to the end of her days were exchanged in the hush of the couple's bedroom. On the last of his two early duty days, he said that, as usual, he would be back for a cup of tea. That would be when the cash deliveries had been completed. And then he was gone.

It was 5.45 a.m.

The detective drove the journey of less than ten minutes through the quiet north side of the city, crossing the Shannon which virtually lapped the rear of the Garda headquarters in Henry Street. At the station he linked up with long-time partner and close friend, Ben O'Sullivan. Armed with their Smith and Wesson revolvers and with the Uzi submachine gun in its case behind them, they moved off from the station. The general post office was just a block away and there they would meet driver and postal service employee of 30 years, Willie Jackson. The three of them must have done that pensions and welfare payments run a thousand times. They were assigned to the west Limerick run; it came round on the first Friday of every month. Ben O'Sullivan was doing the driving. He was always the driver. Jerry had been found to be colour blind and, under Garda regulations, could not be assigned to driving duties. He settled back into the passenger seat. In his pocket was a summons sheet. Somebody had passed it to him and asked if he could make representations to have the matter sorted out. That would have to be for later in the day.

Taking the southern route out of the city with the first stop at Adare, both detectives were pointed towards their native places.

In Ballylongford, Jerry's parents, Johnny and Lizzie, were central figures at the commercial hub of the village. Their family business on Main Street consisted of a grocery and newsagent shop, a hackney cab service and bicycle repairs. The eldest boy in a family of six children, Jerry was fixing bicycles alongside his father by the time he was ten years old. He also had a gift with motors and engines. In his schooldays it was washing machines. From that fascination with engines came his lifelong infatuation with motor cars.

It was the young Garda with the fancy car that caught the fancy of Ann Cuniffe. She was the daughter of a Garda, a Roscommon man who, coincidentally, had been stationed in Ballylongford at one time. He had served in O'Brien's Bridge on the Limerick-Clare border before transferring to the city where he regularly brought daughter Ann to the station to demonstrate the Irish dancing that put her on the theatre stage in Limerick Christmas shows and on the bill with the city's famous comedy duo, Tom and Pascal.

It was dancing that brought them together. The weekly Nurses' Dance at Cruise's Hotel in the heart of Limerick city was the place to be on a Thursday night. A mecca for the young and carefree, dancing was to the music of the city's finest combo, the Monarchs Showband, fronted by John Frawley. Dance-loving hairstylist Ann Cuniffe was there. So was Jerry McCabe. He could dance too. But there was more to him than that. The dashing young Garda who was stationed in tiny Dundrum over the border in county Tipperary had come buzzing into the city in his white MG sportscar with the flamboyant rollback soft top. There was only room for two and they would laugh in later life about the times they combed through the car for coins to pay for petrol when Jerry's monthly salary only lasted a week.

The circumstances that brought Jerry into Garda ranks was also the basis of a career-long bond with his brother-in-law, Pat Kearney.

Pat Kearney from Castleisland was a young Garda, courting Eileen McCabe, when the two men formed an enduring friendship. As the eldest boy from a business family, Jerry had been sent to boarding school in Rockwell College near Cashel in county Tipperary. During that secondary education, the teenager from the Gaelic football stronghold of Kerry was converted to rugby. His secondary schooling complete, Jerry followed the pattern of countless others when he plunged into university student life but barely dipped into his studies in a year at University College, Cork. Back home in Ballylongford, Pat Kearney was a regular visitor to the household and had become virtually part of the family. What Jerry saw of the personable young Garda made an impression and when a new recruitment campaign was announced, Jerry was among the intake at the Templemore Garda Training Centre.

His first posting was Tipperary town. Dundrum was the next stop before the move to Limerick city, where his life as a Garda and his marriage to Ann were to guide the remainder of his life.

It was the attraction of a city and its broad selection of good looking women that brought the handsome young Garda and his low-slung, motorised chariot to Limerick. Although Jerry actually had his eye on a different young woman, once he and Ann met on the dance floor they were smitten. They were soon a couple or, in the parlance of the day, 'doing a steady line'. They would become even closer when Jerry was transferred to the city, and the Limerick links were reinforced by his friendship with Pat Kearney. When Pat married Jerry's sister Eileen, Jerry stood as his best man.

When Jerry and Ann were wed two years after their first meeting, Pat Kearney returned the compliment and was best man, but the closeness did not end there. Jerry's astute, Kerryman father had purchased a house in Limerick's Henry Street. The ground floor became a hairdressing salon first for his daughter and then later for his daughter-in-law, Ann. An upstairs flat in the building became Pat and Eileen Kearney's first home.

When Jerry and Ann married that same flat became their first home. Pat and Eileen had bought their own house in the Corbally suburb of Limerick where, for a time, Des O'Malley was a neighbour.

When their first child, John, was born, Jerry and Ann also moved to a home of their own. Powered by the economic drive provided by Shannon Airport and the build up of overseas investment in industry and hotels that had marked the economic upsurge of the Limerick region, the city was stretching out in all directions. Like a great many members of the Garda force, Jerry, Pat and two of their colleagues pooled their financial resources to buy four sites in the upmarket Castletroy area and, also in keeping with Garda traditions, used their off-duty hours to build their houses.

Never a driver, Ann McCabe found the distance between their new home and the city centre hair salon too much of a burden as she also had a family to look after. Within brisk walking distance of the salon was the house at Avondale Drive which they moved to in the early 1970s and where they would expand their family to five children.

First son John had arrived two years after they married in 1969 and he was followed two years later by Mark. Their third son, Ian, was seven years old before daughter, Stacey, made her appearance. Shortly afterwards the family unit was completed by Ross.

On what was normally a stress free run on the traffic-thin, early morning road to Adare, Jerry McCabe was looking to the future. His holiday break with his sun-worshipping wife was just a week away. Into the bargain, he had been thinking about leaving the Garda ranks and availing of the pensioned retirement option the following year, before striking out in a new enterprise and on the next chapter of his family life.

John, then 27, had followed his father into the Gardaí after his university education and was stationed in Monaghan. Mark was an electrician, married to a nurse and living in Limerick. Ian was 24 and had graduated from the University of Limerick with a degree in public administration.

The final stages of the struggle to rear and educate five children were in sight for the parents. That June morning, 17 year old Stacy was sitting the Leaving Certificate examination at the Salesian Sisters secondary school and her younger brother Ross was also immersed in the stress of examinations, taking the Junior Certificate at Ardscoil Rís.

Jerry's rugby playing days with the famed Clanwilliam Club in Tipperary and with the Garda fifteen, and later involvement with the Na Piarsaigh club, had long been replaced by a passion for golf at both the Castletroy Golf Club and the Garda Golf Society. Otherwise, his off-duty hours were given over to his interest since boyhood in things mechanical, and his natural gifts as a builder.

Within hailing distance of his Garda headquarters, off-duty, Jerry could most regularly be found stretched under a car and tinkering with an engine at a friend's garage in the city docks area. He had recently built a conservatory extension to the family home and, the night before the Adare security run, he was also doing odd jobs. Having worked late at headquarters, instead of heading home he popped over to the fast-food takeaway operated by his brother, Mike, and his wife, Katy. He had promised to fix a faulty window and, once the work was done, he was invited to visit a new bar in the area. He had recently been diagnosed as having an ulcer and Ann had warned him that he could not mix alcohol with his medication. Nevertheless, he joined the company at the new bar where he had a cup of tea.

Tucked in behind the post office truck on the journey of 12 miles to Adare, he could look two weeks ahead to the family holiday that had already been booked. Thinking even further ahead, Jerry and his Special Branch partner of 23 years would regularly chat about the attractions that early retirement could hold for them. Mechanically-gifted Jerry had identified a demand for bathroom shower installation and was mulling over the idea of setting up on his own and taking son, Mark, into the venture with him. But that decision was a little way off because eligibility for retirement would not come round until the following year.

Already 32 years in the Garda force, Ben O'Sullivan was not thinking about retirement even though he had acquired useful skills right through his years of growing up in north Cork. Born into a family of seven boys and three girls, he was named Benjamin which was probably inspired by St Benjamin's holy well at Tullalease near Knockscovane, Meelin, near Newmarket, where he was born. But most of his early life was spent around Liscarroll, near Mallow, where the family moved when he was a toddler.

An athlete and horseman from his youth, he was breaking and training horses by his tenth birthday and, by his mid-teens, was also keenly interested in tug-of-war as a sport.

Ben attended his local national school at Lisgriffin before going on to the Sacred Heart College in Buttevant from where he enlisted in the Gardaí. He was among the second intake of recruits into the new Garda Training Centre at Templemore in north Tipperary. Later to be elevated to college status, the centre opened with 120 recruits in January and Ben was among the 90 grouped in three classes that arrived on 6 May 1964. Although there was no tradition or even links to policing as a career in his family, from the first day of the 22 weeks training he loved the life.

He was posted to Limerick in September, taking up duty at William Street station where he served until 1972.

It did not take long for Garda 15636A Ben O'Sullivan to run into Garda 15860G Jerry McCabe, but when they did meet for the first time, neither knew that the other was a Garda. At the time, Ben was going out with a young woman who shared a house on the Ennis Road with two sisters named McCabe. Once when he called, Jerry was visiting his sisters and they were introduced. But they had to meet as work colleagues before they realised that they shared the same profession.

Their lives in Limerick tended to mirror each other. Jerry married in 1967 and Ben followed down the aisle a year later when he was wed to Barrington Hospital's emergency unit sister, Ann Hanley from Kilcornan in county Limerick. After their September wedding they moved into a semi-detached house in a scheme of just five homes at Old Park Road in the emerging Corbally suburb. The house called

'San Anton' would welcome their first child on the last day of 1969. Like the McCabes, they called their first born John and, in later years, he was joined by three girls, Marianne, Evelyn and Aoife.

While setting up home, Ben O'Sullivan was also lending his considerable strength to one of the favoured sports of sports-mad Limerick. He joined St Michael's Rowing Club, coming through the ranks from maiden to junior and then senior class. He was a member of the Limerick Garda crews that won the fours and eights at the 1969 Garda championships. A year later he was even prouder to be part of the Limerick eight that went to Islandbridge and bested the Dublin crew that had basked in the prestigious international events at the high profile Henley Regatta in England. He continued his involvement with tug-of-war events as a coach and official, travelling throughout the country. He blended work with his favourite sport when he coached a Limerick Garda women's tug-of-war team to win the Garda sports championship at Dublin's Billy Morton Stadium in Santry in 1989.

Once they got together when they both joined the Special Branch detective unit, Ben and Jerry did everything together. They were inseparable in working, leisure and social life. Every passing day brought them closer together. Both found that they had a great deal in common with their partner, including manual activities. Both were able builders and enhanced their houses with their own work. Both could fall back on what they had learned from their respective fathers. Jerry was mechanical. Ben was at ease with horses and cattle. Ben could also butcher a beast, and on those occasions he and Jerry liked to work as a unit. When the family freezers were to be topped up, Ben carved the carcasses and Jerry wrapped and packed the joints.

Their move up to detective rank on 21 November 1972 marked the start of a new phase in their careers and lives as the island of Ireland headed into more than three decades of killing and carnage spilling over from the civil rights campaigns and subsequent, brutal responses which rapidly flared into armed conflict.

They were part of a four man unit, but it almost invariably happened that they operated together. They investigated serious crime, tracked and gathered intelligence on subversive activity and acted as security guards on movements of money. The post office cash in transit and bank transfers could regularly number three in a working day. On the west Limerick run, the detectives and post office driver, Willie Jackson, were old hands. Not one of them had ever come under attack before.

As they arrived in Adare, the time was 6.50 a.m.

Back home at Avondale Drive, Ann McCabe was getting her two youngest sorted out for the State exams that were dominating family life. The phone rang. A concerned friend was on the line. She had just heard a radio newsflash that two Gardaí had been injured in Adare. Jerry was in Adare. Ann McCabe immediately rang Henry Street Garda headquarters. All the lines were engaged. Something very serious was happening. She hardly had time to think, or allow herself think. Then the doorbell was ringing. She assumed it was school friends calling for her two examination students on their way to the exam halls.

When she opened the door, Ann McCabe was faced by a man who she did not know. He was accompanied by a woman Garda. The man was John Kerin, newly promoted to the rank of Inspector and assigned to the Garda regional headquarters at Henry Street. On his first day in the new post, he had to go the home of a woman he did not know to inform her that her detective husband had been shot dead. It was Inspector Kerin who would lead the hunt for the killers and bring them to the dock of the Special Criminal Court in Dublin on charges of capital murder.

What Inspector Kerin had to say was not really comprehensible to Ann McCabe. Bewildered, confused and dazed, she collapsed in her hallway. Nevertheless, four year later she would recall, 'For as long as I live, I will never forget the screams of Stacey as she ran up the stairs.'

Chapter 3

The Kalashnikov assault rifle had been on the guerilla warfare and revolutionary scene throughout the globe for almost 50 years before it became part of Adare infamy. Ranked by the specialists of the ballistics world as the ideal small arm, the AK-47, as it is generally known, is favoured by subversives because of its simplicity of operation and maintenance, its ruggedness and its reliability even in the worst conditions.

Developed by the Russian army sergeant Mikhail Kalashnikov during hospital recuperation from war wounds in the latter years of World War II, the AK-47 named after him was modified and improved through the decades so that the most used version from the 1980s-90s era was the AKM, or the 'Modern' model. Easy to handle and carry, without its magazine the AK-47 weighs nine and a half pounds or just over four kilograms. The even lighter AKM weighs just shy of half a stone at marginally under seven pounds, or 3.14 kilograms.

Since its appearance in 1947 more than 90 million Kalashnikov rifles have been manufactured. It was widely exported to pro-Soviet countries and was manufactured under license in many of the communist satellite countries and countries regarded as friendly by the Soviet Union regime.

More than 1,000 Kalashnikovs came into the hands of the IRA in the mid-1980s as part of the unprecedented demonstration of support for the war against imperialist interests by the Libyan revolutionary leader, Colonel Ghadafi, in retaliation for the US bombing of Tripoli that had targeted him.

The offer of enormous military equipment could not have come at a better time for the IRA. The weapons pipeline from the USA, which had directed an estimated 300 guns per year and over a million rounds of ammunition to the Provisional IRA in the 1970s, had been smashed in a crackdown by the US authorities in 1981. Supply of arms to the IRA arsenals was also hit in an FBI 'sting' operation in 1982 when an attempt to buy a missile was exposed by agents posing as arms dealers. Two years later came a body blow to the IRA, and an enormous lift for the prestige of the security authorities in the Republic, when the *Marita Ann* gun running was spectacularly foiled. The ship was captured off the south-west coast. Accompanying the deadly cargo, which was nearing his Kerry home county, was Martin Ferris, the republican activist and future member of the Dáil.

But gun running was to move into a different league with the offer from the Libyan intelligence service to supply 300 tons of weapons of war. With a republican supporter in Bray, county Wicklow, as the go-between, the IRA cut a deal with one-time high profile holiday package operator, Adrian Hopkins, whose Bray Travel operation had collapsed with losses running to over a million pounds. He was to provide and captain the vessel, and be paid £50,000 for each trip to the Mediterranean where IRA crew would rendezvous with a Libyan ship for transfer of cargo.

On the first test-run with a small consignment, the *Casamara* fishing boat brought seven tons of arms. Offloaded out from the Wicklow coast and moved by outboard-powered dinghies to Clogga Strand, the first shipment included Kalashnikov rifles as well as Taurus automatic pistols. 100 Kalashnikovs were included in the second shipment two months later at the end of the summer of 1985. On that run the consignment had been increased to ten tons, and also included general purpose machine guns, Webley revolvers and several tons of ammunition.

It would take nine months before the next shipment came through in July 1986 with an even bigger cargo. With a name change to *Kula*, the fishing boat brought in 14 tons of weapons that included a first delivery of SAM-7 missiles which the IRA coveted for use against British military helicopter patrols.

But that was just the forerunner of the bumper cargo which was to be brought ashore in the last quarter of 1986. Aboard a former oil rig service vessel, which had been renamed *Villa*, was a cargo of over 100 tons of weapons and five tons of the Semtex plastic explosive that would cause mayhem and slaughter in the years ahead. In addition to more than 60 machine guns, over a million rounds of ammunition, more surface to air missiles, plus rocket launchers and grenades, the shipment included 1,200 Kalashnikov assault rifles.

The massive build up of the IRA arsenal, and the addition of the most up to date weaponry and explosives, only came to light when the *Eksund* was intercepted off the French coast in October 1987. From an international collaboration of security and intelligence organisations, a shipment that was larger than all the other four together was halted.

But while the security forces were jubilant about the capture of the 150 tons of military equipment, including a further 1,000 Kalashnikovs, a series of initiatives were to be launched that aimed to track down the hiding places and bunkers where the previous four deliveries had been stashed away.

In the years that followed, an estimated 600 of the Romanian-manufactured AKMs from the Libya shipments would be seized in RUC and Garda operations.

Due to the magnitude of the arms and armaments that came from Libya, the Provisional IRA took predictable precautions to maintain the tightest secrecy and security concerning the whereabouts of the supplies. In the mid-1980s Micky McKevitt had become the IRA Quartermaster General whose responsibilities included supply of weapons, equipment and money to active service volunteers. He was also entrusted with the task of bringing the Libyan arms into the country and distributing the weaponry to hiding places in the Republic, especially the western part of the country. McKevitt used a hand-picked group to preserve confidentiality and, as Quartermaster General, he would have also had a close relationship of mutual trust with the IRA group operating out of Patrickswell in county Limerick. This group specialised in fundraising operations to meet the cost of the armed struggle, which was then variously estimated at somewhere between £8-10 million a year.

Kalashnikov rifles and Semtex turned up in Patrickswell and Limerick city in the nationwide sweeps by the security forces for arms after the capture of the *Eksund* netted information about the earlier shipments.

In March 1988, three Kalashnikovs fitted with telescopic sights were seized in Patrickswell along with revolvers, rifles and shotguns, a quantity of Semtex with trip switches and three 150-page training manuals.

In a Limerick city raid in May 1990, further Kalashnikovs, a quantity of Semtex, handguns and ammunition were uncovered.

That there were more than enough Kalashnikovs to go round would be demonstrated as the distinctive assault rifles were brandished, and in a number of cases fired, during armed robberies, and when more than one turned up during the hunt for the Adare killers.

Durable without being heavy, dependable with minimum maintenance, the Kalashnikov was the ideal weapon for subversives needing to hit and run. The effectiveness of the assault rifle was based on the design by a front line soldier that built in all the features that a military marksman would want.

Firing copper-plated bullets from what was usually a magazine holding 30 rounds, its devastating power was tested and attested to in evidence put before the Adare killing trial.

Fitted with a lever which allows shots to be fired in semi-automatic or automatic mode, the tests carried out by Garda ballistics experts showed that, in full automatic mode, 15 rounds could be fired in less than two seconds.

15 rounds were blazed at the Garda escort car where detectives McCabe and O'Sullivan were sitting on that June morning in 1996. Fired from a roadside position, opposite driver Ben O'Sullivan, five shots went wide and three were stopped by the frame of the vehicle on the driver's side.

Up to five bullets would exit on Jerry McCabe's passenger side.

Three bullets hit Detective McCabe. His spine was severed. In less than two seconds he was dead.

Chapter 4

The organisation of the 'well planned operation', as the abortive Adare raid was described to the Special Criminal Court, can be reconstructed through evidence put before the court as well as other records and official accounts.

While the advance planning would involve a great deal more than the routine stealing of the vehicles involved a week before the raid, the Adare operation was very different to the 30-odd robberies that Gardaí reckoned had been carried out by the IRA group in previous years. Besides the co-ordinated movement of IRA volunteers, weapons and transport and synchronised arrangements for support personnel and safe houses, the fundraising activity was resuming after a ceasefire that had held for 15 months up to February of that year.

Because the IRA group masterminded from Patrickswell was of vital fundraising importance, the leaders of the group were close to the IRA Quartermaster General. His prime duties were to equip and finance the paramilitaries. From 1985 that position within the IRA command structure was held by Micky McKevitt, who was prominently identified with those inside the IRA who opposed the ceasefire. Variously termed a 'cessation' by Sinn Féin and the 'sos' (pronounced *suss*) or 'pause' in IRA parlance, the Quartermaster General was an advocate of a return to the armed struggle. He and his wife, Bernadette, the sister of the first H-Blocks hunger striker to die, Bobby Sands, were to break away and form alternative structures when the peace process and ceasefire were brought back on track.

The ceasefire that had started at the end of the summer of 1994 was brought to a headline-capturing end with the devastating explosion that killed two and caused damage estimated at around £100 million sterling at London's Canary Wharf. That explosion on 9 February was caused by a massive truck-bomb which had been built in south Armagh, then smuggled into England and the underground car park of the six storey office block, where it was detonated. Because of the timetable involved, it was therefore estimated that the go ahead for the ceasefire to be blown away had been given by the ruling IRA Army Council at least two months before. That would have been in the closing months of 1995.

That preparations for the resumption of fundraising raids to finance the armed struggle were also getting under way in the Limerick and north Munster area became clear at the end of 1995.

As a result of intelligence gathering by the security forces, 'Operation Mid-West' was activated in December which foiled preparations for a major raid on a cash in transit shipment.

Gardaí seized two trucks, a van and a saloon car close to the Limerick-Cork border near Charleville shortly before Christmas. The Gardaí followed up with searches and seizure of up to a dozen further vehicles.

That subversive elements involved in fundraising were under surveillance was also indicated towards the end of February 1996 when a group of men were detained by Gardaí in Dublin. Named after arrest in the South Circular Road area of Dublin was Pearse McCauley, who was on bail on a British extradition warrant. With him were four men, two from Patrickswell and two from Cavan. They were detained under the Offences against the State Act and questioned by Special Branch detectives at the Bridewell Garda station. Having been held for 36 hours, they were released while a file relating to a car stolen in Monaghan was prepared for the Director of Public Prosecutions.

Among the vehicles seized by Gardaí in 'Operation Mid-West' were a number of Mitsubishi models. Two Mitsubishis were to feature prominently in the Adare robbery.

A Mitsubishi Pajero jeep was stolen from outside the home of Michael Cleary in Rathfarnham, Dublin, a week before the Adare raid on 31 May. Four days later the second vehicle was stolen, again in Dublin. Secondary school teacher Kathleen O'Donnell had driven her Mitsubishi Lancer across the country from her home in Ballina, county Mayo, to the capital where she was to supervise Leaving Certificate examinations. She parked outside the house in Sandymount where she was staying but next morning, on 4 June, the car was gone. She had taken ownership of the new Lancer just 12 days before.

The black Pajero jeep emblazoned with 'Country Gardens' on its bonnet would serve as the heavyweight ramming vehicle, and the speedy and easy to handle silver Lancer as the getaway car. Both vehicles had been fitted with false number plates. While the false registrations were for Dublin, they would not attract any special attention around the area of Adare. As the Limerick gateway to the south-west holiday resorts of Kerry and west Cork, vehicles from outside the area were a routine sight and were almost ever present in Adare itself as the weddings capital of the country.

The two vehicles turned up in the car park of a bar on the Dublin approach to Limerick city on the eve of the Adare raid.

John Quinn, a carpenter who worked in the construction business with his brother, was regarded by Gardaí as a 'close associate' of the IRA group centred in his home place of Patrickswell. Later, he would be described to the Special Criminal Court as a 'messenger' for his IRA associates.

Two weeks before the raid, Quinn had been approached by Kevin Walsh and asked to make himself available for an upcoming job and to buy plastic ties. Quinn paid £48 out of his own pocket for the ties, which he understood would be used to restrain people. He also understood that the job was to be a post office raid.

At the time Quinn was living with Eleanor Harty who was estranged from her husband. They first met in 1993 and had been in a relationship from November of that year with Quinn living on her farm.

On the eve of the raid, Quinn asked to borrow her car and said he had to go to Mullingar to collect a man who was ill. He left the farmhouse at around 9.30 at night, returning at approximately 2 a.m.

Quinn had been instructed to pick up a passenger close to a garage in Rathkeale. He then drove with Kevin Walsh, taking minor roads to skirt Limerick and carry them from the southern approach to the city to the northern Dublin road area. There, various elements of the next morning's operation were brought together. Senior IRA figures went over the plan for the cash robbery. They met in Herbert's Bar on the Dublin road out of Limerick. Further down the road, on the approach to the city, in the car park of a bar and restaurant that traded under the name of MJ Finnegan's, they linked up to take charge of the stolen Pajero and Lancer vehicles.

Quinn recognised Pearse McCauley and others who he knew to be senior IRA men, two of whom were 'higher than Kevin [Walsh]'. Quinn heard them discussing tactics for the raid. He heard one man tell Kevin Walsh that there was to be no ramming because it was too dangerous a tactic and would not be sanctioned. But another man stated that everything had been 'okayed from the top' and Walsh himself said it would be fine.

Quinn was then instructed to take the 'pilot' role in leading the vehicles back to Patrickswell, with Walsh driving the Pajero, followed by the Lancer. On their way back, they passed the Patrickswell Garda patrol car.

Quinn then followed instructions to buy diesel for the jeep. He was also told where to pick up a bag in a laneway. The bag contained ammunition clips for a Kalashnikov AK 47. He brought the bag to Kevin Walsh's parental home and threw it over a door.

Back in Patrickswell, the IRA men went uninvited into the home shared by Kevin Walsh's sister, Sally, and their father, Patrick. The Pajero jeep was parked in the yard. Moving in and out of the house at Lurriga, Patrickswell, during the night were Kevin Walsh, Pearse McCauley, Jerry Sheehy, Michael O'Neill and Gerry Roche. O'Neill passed some time cleaning weapons. The IRA men brought with them a bag with four rifles and magazines, and other arms included a sawn-off, double barrel shotgun and a number of handguns.

Before Detective Jerry McCabe and his partner Detective Ben O'Sullivan started into their 6 a.m. shift, the IRA men were up and about in Adare. One of their number, identified by his ginger hair, was seen sitting on a wall near the Lantern Lodge outside Adare at 5.30 in the morning when a convoy of vehicles drive through the village. On that same morning another witness encountered the silver Mitsubishi Lancer and the getaway driver. The witness saw the car was driven by a man with a moustache and brownish hair.

The post office truck, with £80,000 on board, had left the general post office in Limerick at 6.30 a.m., escorted by the blue Ford Mondeo unmarked Garda escort car. The two vehicles pulled in to the side of Adare's wide main street outside the post office at 6.50 a.m.

In Kilmallock two years previously, the post office vehicle was rammed. This time it was the Garda escort car that the raiders hit.

Immediately after the black Pajero crashed into the blue Ford Mondeo, a number of figures emerged wearing balaclavas and paramilitary green and black battle dress, and carrying Kalashnikov rifles. The armed men took up positions on each side of the Garda car. It was then that the still Adare morning was shattered by a burst of automatic gunfire directed into the driver's side of the escort vehicle, spraying thousands of bits of metal in all directions as the bullets struck the frame of the Garda car, hitting both detectives and narrowly missing the raider on the other side of the car.

The post office SDS truck was fitted with a new cage security system. Consequently, it would have taken a period of at least ten minutes, and up to 20 minutes, to seize all the money. So, according to An Post, the only feasible way in which the raiders could have taken the cash was to take the truck.

But no attempt was made to either get at the money or take the truck. Instead, the getaway car, the silver Mitsubishi Lancer, came up so fast alongside the other vehicles at the scene of the shooting that it also grazed the side of one of the halted vehicles. Four men jumped into the getaway car, driven by a figure in a balaclava, and sped away, abandoning the Lancer about eight miles outside the town. Later, found in the Lancer was an incendiary device which Gardaí associated with IRA operations. Normally used to burn out vehicles and destroy possible clues and leads, the incendiary device had not been activated. A similar device was found in the black Pajero, abandoned in the Adare street, behind the car where one detective was slumped dead in his seat and another was critically wounded.

The Lancer that had taken the IRA men from the scene was driven to Morenane Wood near Croom which was deeper into county Limerick. With Garda roadblocks and checkpoints going up within minutes of the fatal shooting, the raiders switched to a car which would not be identified by witnesses in Adare.

Due to the roundabout route of the getaway, it was nearly two hours before the five men arrived at the home of farmer John Harty, a bachelor who led a quiet solitary life at Toomevara in county Tipperary. The IRA men told the owner that they wanted to stay at the house. Two of the men had military-style rifles, another carried a shotgun, and a fourth was armed with a pistol. The farmer was given instructions for boiler suits and gloves to be burned and for the wood stock to be sawn off the rifle. They also told the farmer that the weapons would be collected at a later date.

The prime reason why the shooting dead of Jerry McCabe remains an 'open file' with the Garda authorities is the knowledge that a much larger number of people were complicit in the Adare raid than those actually on the scene. In such IRA operations a variety of people were usually used for a variety of tasks. Furthermore, the co-ordination of such raids also involved deployment of IRA volunteers from different areas and in roundabout movements to minimise advance detection. So, individual IRA volunteers could be ordered to rendezvous at particular places at certain times. There, they may be given further orders that would take them miles away from the destination they were initially ordered to. When a raiding party was eventually assembled, some of the IRA volunteers could be meeting for the first time. Around the raiding party, other clandestine actions had to be carried out. Vehicles had to be moved into the target area and hidden from public view. Overnight accommodation and other 'safe house' refuges had to be organised. Most of all, independent of the movements of the raiding group, weapons had to be moved in and out of the area.

On Saturday, 8 June, the day after the Adare killing, a member of the IRA living in the midlands received a telephone call from a superior and was directed to the Toomevara farm outside Nenagh. He was to check if the gang was still there. There, he found that the men had gone but left their weapons behind. It was not until the Thursday of the following week, six days after the killing, that he was instructed to return to the farm to recover the arms. On his arrival, early that morning, the farmer moved his tractor and took the guns and a plastic bag out of the trailer box. The weapons were transported in the boot of the IRA man's car to a pre-arranged pick-up point, where he left the deadly delivery.

Chapter 5

It was the moment of dread, the nightmarish realisation of every terror and foreboding.

'Oh Jesus, Jerry!' Ben O'Sullivan gasped when he saw the black Pajero jeep looming larger and larger in the rear view mirror and clearly not reducing speed. He knew immediately what was happening when he saw that the bulky figures of the driver and front seat passenger had their heads covered by balaclavas.

The Pajero slammed into the rear of the unmarked blue Ford Mondeo with such force that Ben O'Sullivan's arm was broken. On the street in front of them, driver Willie Jackson was in the act of opening up the back of the post office truck. He heard the crash, turned and saw three masked and armed men. He thought he was about to die. Despite the dazed confusion inside the Garda car, Ben O'Sullivan nevertheless saw two figures jump from the Pajero and move smartly up on each side of the Garda escort car. Their faces covered, they were wearing battledress. He recognised the weapons as Kalashnikov assault rifles.

It was not the first time that Ben O'Sullivan had faced a man with a gun. On three previous occasions he had confronted an armed man. Two of those happened out of public view during routine investigations. One case involved a man with a shotgun. In the second a rifle was involved. The third case took place on a public road in daylight in a built up area of Limerick city, and won him a bravery award. That was in 1992 when he took on a man armed with a loaded shotgun which had the safety catch off. The detective physically tackled the man, charging at him rugby-style and crashing into him at upper body level. They both fell to the ground where the gunman was overpowered. Ben's bravery was recognised with the award of a gold Scott Medal from the Garda force and a civic reception salute from the Mayor and Corporation of Limerick.

But now there were gunmen with automatic weapons on each side of the car in which the detective and his partner were trapped. They had no time to draw the .38 Smith and Wesson revolvers in their belts or reach for the Uzi submachine gun which was behind them, still in its case, not loaded and with its safety catch on.

Then the gunman on Ben O'Sullivan's side of the car opened fire.

Ten of the 15 bullets blasted through the driver's window and into the confined compartment of the car. Three shots ended up lodged in different parts of the driver's side of the car. Up to five bullets finished up or exited on the passenger side of the car.

As told to the Special Criminal Court in 1999, the bullets passing through the car broke up into tiny projectiles, with a hail of bullet pieces hurtling and splintering through the compartment, causing massive damage to the occupants and also to the car.

His arm already broken by the ramming impact, Ben O'Sullivan was first hit in the right shoulder. One of the two bullets exited half an inch from his spinal column, and the other halfway through his shoulder blade. The second blast blew his hands off the steering wheel, forcing him bodily onto the handbrake on his left as the driver's window shattered around him. The fingers and thumb of his left hand were wounded, as well as two fingers of his right hand. He suffered a bullet wound below his right eye, wounds on each side of his head and a bullet graze on his right thigh.

On the passenger side, Jerry McCabe had also been hit. Two bullets pierced his back. One struck him in the right shoulder fracturing the shoulder blade. Another entered through the back of his right upper arm. The killer shot also entered through his back. The bullet shattered his eighth rib and vertebrae, severing his spinal column before tearing into his lungs and lacerating the pulmonary vein and aorta, the main vessel carrying blood from the heart to the rest of the body. The bullet exited through the left side of his back.

Although grievously wounded himself, in the aftershock of the automatic gunfire that had splintered and spewed torrents of terror inside the car, Ben O'Sullivan's first thought was for his partner and friend.

When the shooting stopped, he could hear shouting but could not make out what was being said. He called out, 'Jerry, Jerry, Jerry.' But there was no response. He could see that his companion was 'in great difficulty', as the detective would recall to the Special Criminal Court.

He saw that Jerry's hand was contorting and his arm was turning blue. Although both of Ben's hands were severely wounded and bleeding, he put the small finger of his left hand onto Jerry's wrist.

There was no pulse.

'Death would have been very rapid,' the assistant state pathologist, Dr Margaret Bolster, would say in her evidence to the Special Criminal Court. Having conducted a post mortem examination of his body, her conclusions were that Jerry McCabe's death was caused by haemorrhage, shock and lacerations of the lungs due to a gunshot wound to the back of the thorax.

Chapter 6

'The gang who murdered Detective Garda Jerry McCabe and wounded Detective Garda Ben O'Sullivan also blasted away whatever pretence terrorism might have had to anything approaching popular support on Shannonside.'

The editorial in *The Limerick Leader* was prophetic as the adopted city home of the detectives and the region it serves was numbed and shocked beyond words by the atrocity in Adare.

'The IRA and Sinn Féin have moved to distance themselves from the crime,' the editorial noted. 'They have not moved far enough. They do not condone it but nor do they condemn it.'

'This nauseating ambivalence from the very people who profess belief in the peace process has caused deep offence in Limerick,' added the editorial in understatement of the rage that gripped the city and county.

Sinn Féin and the IRA were nowhere to be seen or heard as Limerick delivered its answer on the streets and in the churches.

Sunday massgoers in the Catholic churches of the diocese of Limerick heard an appeal from their Bishop, Donal Murray, for co-operation with the Garda investigation. At all Church of Ireland services, a statement from Bishop Edward Darling expressed 'horror and revulsion at a dastardly and murderous attack'. The Bishop's statement added, 'this criminal incident has naturally disturbed the whole of our community.'

That Sunday night 20,000 people queued from 6.00 p.m. until midnight to pay their respects and express their solidarity with the widow and family of Detective Jerry McCabe. Government representatives who joined in the expression of condolences at Thompson's funeral home in the Thomas Street heart of Limerick were led by the Tánaiste and Minister for Foreign Affairs, Dick Spring, leader of the Labour Party and Dáil deputy for the dead detective's native north Kerry. With him were the Minister for Justice, Nora Owen, of the Fine Gael majority partner in government, and the Labour Minister of State, Joan Burton.

The thousands who had assembled outside the funeral home were held up for some time when Ann McCabe and her extended family were detained back at the McCabe home on the north side of the city.

That Sunday afternoon a message had come through to the office of Mayor Jim Kemmy, Alderman and Dáil deputy, that the American Ambassador, Ms Jean Kennedy Smith, was on her way to Limerick to share the family grief that her own family had twice suffered with the assassinations of her brothers, President John F Kennedy and presidential candidate, Robert Kennedy.

The Ambassador arrived without fanfare, with no trappings of her office and no obvious security presence or official retinue. At the Avondale Drive home, she went directly to the kitchen to join and console the woman adrift in a black hole of loss and shock. An enduring bond was formed. The Ambassador joined the grieving family in the living room, sitting among them for three hours. So many McCabes were in the house that she memorably commented that she was reminded of the Kennedy home. Before departing, she presented Ann McCabe with the rosary beads belonging to her mother, Mrs Rose Kennedy, matriarch of the Kennedy clan that had its Camelot dreams shattered by gunmen's bullets.

President Mary Robinson and the leader of the Government, Taoiseach John Bruton, were in the congregation at the funeral Mass in the Church of the Holy Rosary on the Ennis Road where the McCabes were familiar figures.

Tens of thousands lined the route as uniformed Gardaí left an indelible impression on city memory as they honoured their fellow officer. In ceremonial march, with their polished toecaps tapping out a slow, synchronised tattoo, 400 Gardaí, led by their Commissioner and augmented by the armed forces, crossed the elegant five arches of Sarsfield Bridge that had opened up the northern side of the Shannon from 1835, continuing along the mute Ennis Road.

The middle sons in the McCabe family of four sons and a daughter, 25 year old Mark and 24 year old Ian, read the lessons. The funeral Mass took place in the unique wooden church, different from any other in a city of churches, and celebrated for its artistic and heritage importance.

Under the distinctive bell tower and surrounded by uplifting works of art, the McCabe family funeral was conducted amid the combined voices of the Garda choir and solos by singer and harpist, Muirne Hurley. Muirne had sung at Jerry McCabe's 50th birthday two years earlier and she sang his favourite, 'Nedin', during the funeral Mass. Choir and congregation joined in the chorus when she sang the hymn 'Be Not Afraid'. Among the crunch of media personnel in the thronged church was Veronica Guerin, star crime and investigative journalist with the *Sunday Independent*. She would later confide that she too would like 'Be Not Afraid' to be sung at her funeral which, tragically, was only a matter of weeks away. She was gunned down in broad daylight as she drove back to her Dublin workplace on 26 June.

It was the show of feeling from the ordinary people of Limerick which would remain with Ann McCabe. Some years later at the unveiling of the memorial bust of her husband, she shared her thoughts with the Gardaí and distinguished guests at Henry Street Garda headquarters:

> *On that sad day when Jerry's funeral passed through the streets of Limerick, thousands of people, people who had never met either Jerry or myself, stopped what they were doing, came out of shops and places of business and stood in silence as the cortège passed them by. At a time of deep personal anguish, this gesture by ordinary decent people was intensely moving and comforting to my family and myself. It was as if, by their silence and by their sheer numbers, the people of Limerick were saying that they had had enough and that they were unwilling to give any form of support to crimes like this, no matter what their so-called political motivation might be.*

Over on the other side of the city, Detective Garda Ben O'Sullivan had a visitor to his bedside in the intensive care unit of Limerick Regional Hospital. While most of Limerick city and county seemed to be with the McCabes at Our Lady of the Rosary Church, Detective O'Sullivan was not alone with his pain and his thoughts. He did not know his visitor. He was Rev Michael Nuttall, Church of Ireland Archdeacon of the widely scattered diocese centred on its city cathedral at the heart of Limerick. But the Archdeacon lived in Adare. Throughout the two hours of the funeral Mass and burial of his partner and great friend, Ben O'Sullivan was spared the lonely desolation of permanent loss.

His bodily pain was being controlled by medication. Besides the gaping holes in his shoulder and back where the Kalashnikov bullets had torn and twisted in and out of his body, the shooting had been at such close range that the charge had also invaded his body. That, in the words of his medical team, had 'fried the flesh', causing excruciating suffering which the detective would only recall as beyond the most extreme pain. A knuckle on one of the fingers of his left hand had been blasted away, and one finger of his right hand no longer had a middle joint.

Following the funeral Mass and interment, John McCabe, the new man at the head of the family, and a Garda like his father, issued a statement on behalf of himself, his only sister and three brothers. The statement read:

> *Jerry will always be remembered as a friend, a colleague and member of the Garda Síochána, but for us, his family, he will always be remembered as the most wonderful husband and father. Dad's deep and abiding love for his children was obvious to everybody. Each one of us always felt very special to him and, as we grew, our relationship with him developed into one of friendship as well as of family. I know I speak for my sister and brothers when I say that we have a tremendous pride in everything Dad did, from career to golf to conservatory construction. As adults, we now see that who we have become results from many years of love, patience and hard work by both Mom and Dad. Whatever they did, they were always together for us, and we know for many of you they have been a wonderful example of a couple in love and united.*

Chapter 7

Adare was not the first bungled effort by armed IRA robbers. Neither was it the first botched paramilitary action to cost a life. For one of the Adare raiders, it was the second abortive action in which a life was lost. The two deadly events took place less than 50 miles and eight years apart. But the first cast a very long shadow over the Adare killing of Jerry McCabe.

It was the first Friday in May of 1988 and was remembered in those terms of Catholic Church observance by Mary Kelly, post mistress at the tiny hamlet of Caher in the hill country of east Clare. Her rustic post office operated from the ground floor of her home which was tucked away to the side of a little cluster of three or four homes, looking out on and within earshot of the lapping waters of Lough Graney.

The largest lake in east Clare, and the most extensive expanse of inland water inside the county bounds, the awesome beauty of Lough Graney is part of Irish literary lore. Cupped between forested mountains and elevated bogland stretched between the counties of Clare and Galway, the lake is celebrated as the inspiration of a milestone classic of Gaelic literature.

Combining breathtaking vistas with serene calm, the lakeshore provided the wild walking routes and still resting places where poet Brian Merriman composed *The Midnight Court*. Merriman was a teacher in the village of Feakle about five miles over the hills from Lough Graney. *The Midnight Court* is remarkable not simply for its literary merit but holds a unique place in Irish social history. Comfortably serving as a verse-drama, *Midnight Court* ridicules and lampoons the conventions and sexual repression of a priest-ridden society that was recognisable two centuries after Merriman first penned it. The earthy language in which the sexual frustration of Irish womanhood was expressed as they put their menfolk on trial in the midnight sitting of a fairy court, ensured that the exceptional work of literature was banned both in its original Irish and translations, until the easing of puritan censorship that characterised Ireland until the liberal 1960s.

The solitude and undisturbed rural isolation that made such an impression on Merriman also had instinctive appeal for people and activities demanding absolute secrecy. Like many other remote tracts in all parts of the country, the lonely unfrequented areas, with their dense natural cover and thinly-spread Garda manpower, were ideal for secret training and exercises. From the area's hunting haunts, the sound of gunfire caused no alarm or curiosity. And in the east Clare area, active service IRA volunteers could feel at home.

Strongly nationalistic, east Clare's republican credentials were also well established. Up to his death in 1982, the most prominent local politician in east Clare was Dr Bill Loughnane, an unashamedly outspoken supporter of the armed struggle. A heroic, larger than life figure, the former army officer, local doctor, All-Ireland winning hurler and fiddle player with the acclaimed Tulla Céilí Band, made no secret of his support for 'the boys' when their shadowy movements were occasionally happened on in the area. In his support for the staunchly republican former Fianna Fáil Minister, Neil Blaney, and public criticism of northern policy, he was instrumental in bringing down Taoiseach, Jack Lynch, who resigned in 1979 to be succeeded by the minister he sacked along with Blaney in the 1970 Arms Crisis, Charles Haughey.

Dr Bill's Feakle home also had a place in the history books, both for peace making and armed struggle. It was the Smyth Village Hotel, in the village of Feakle, where the IRA leadership met in secret weekend session with Churchmen of various denominations from the North in 1974, to talk about how peace might be brought about. In that same period, Harry Duggan from Feakle was a member of the IRA unit which killed 16 and maimed dozens more in a bombing campaign in England over 1973-74 that included the Guildford and Woolwich bombings. Accredited as an active service volunteer with the mid-Ulster IRA, Harry Duggan had been active on the border area before being posted on the bombing mission in England along with fellow Clareman, Joe O'Connell, Eddie Butler from neighbouring county Limerick and Hugh Doherty, brother of Pat

Doherty who subsequently became vice president of Sinn Féin. The four were cornered and jailed after a siege when they held a couple hostage in a London block of flats which gave the bomber quartet the title 'The Balcombe Street Gang'. Sentenced to 47 life sentences, a lengthy campaign for their transfer to Irish prisons was fruitless until the 1990s peace process. When released on parole to mark the Good Friday Agreement shortly after their relocation to Ireland, the televised proceedings of the 1998 Sinn Féin Ard Fheis were brought to a standstill when the four were given an ecstatic reception by the party conference delegates who had risen to their feet when called on to welcome the 'Balcombe Street Four' as they paraded onto the platform to be embraced by the party leadership.

It was no surprise to Mary Kelly when her Caher post office was the target for an armed hold up. She had been waiting for it. She had been preparing for it.

She had calculated that it was only a matter of time before Caher would be added to the map charting where bank, payroll and post office armed robberies had taken place throughout the country. She was a woman alone in what could rank among the most isolated post offices in the country. But Mary Kelly was a different kind of woman.

The private courier vehicle hired for the post office deliveries had made three other calls in east Clare before delivering £8,000 to Caher for distribution in three townlands of pension and other state payments. The truck was escorted by a Garda car from Killaloe with two members of the Gardaí, one of whom was armed.

The delivery vehicles had moved on over the heights of Maghera to the main concentration of population in Feakle when she saw him.

Through the window Mary Kelly spied a lone man wearing a balaclava over his face and armed with a weapon. She stepped out to the door in an attempt to shut him out. The masked man demanded 'give me the money!' and pushed the barrel of the weapon towards her. It would later be related to the media that Mary Kelly screamed and shouted. She was not the kind of woman to scream. She could certainly shout because she was more than capable of a verbal assault, that was not short on rough language, which could stop any man in his tracks, including an armed robber.

Carrying across the placid water of Lough Graney may have been a screech. But that would have been the pitch of the voice rather than a cry of panic. With the distraction of her shouts, Mary reached out and pulled the weapon from the raider. He turned and ran.

The postmistress made an immediate call to Feakle post office. Her fear was that, having missed out on takings at Caher, the raider or raiders would choose a new target. In Feakle, the delivery was being made and the Garda car turned round and headed back for Caher.

In the meantime, Mary Kelly had stashed the post office money in one of the hiding places that she had used for years. Legend has it that she would often keep thousands in currency notes in her fridge.

With the weapon that had been torn from the raider's hands, she took off over nearby lanes to get herself out of the way.

The raider who had come back empty handed, without the money or his weapon, rejoined an accomplice in a white Opel van. They had overnighted in the area, hiding a second car, a red Ford Fiesta, close to a quarry for an early morning raid and getaway with a switch of vehicles to aid the escape.

The would-be robbers first returned to the post office in Caher that Mary Kelly had abandoned. There they ransacked the office but failed to find the money. But the money was there. It was hidden in the best possible way, almost open to view, in a cardboard carton under the counter, where it sat among discarded documents and other waste.

Just as Mary had anticipated, the two raiders then headed towards Feakle. But at the same time the Garda car was on its way back towards Caher. They confronted each other somewhere in the middle. The raiders were seen to be armed and the driver was wearing a balaclava. The Gardaí called on them to lay down the arms and surrender. Shots were exchanged.

Armed detectives are called on very rarely to use their firearms. Besides their yearly arms practice sessions, many never fire a shot in the course of their duty. It was the misfortune of the Caher raiders that the armed detective was a seasoned hunter and a sharpshooter, regarded as one of the top marksmen in the entire Garda force.

Having fired over the heads of the raiders as an initial warning, when fire was returned, the detective aimed for a disabling shot. Instead one raider was hit in the head and Hugh Hehir, an IRA active service volunteer for 20 of his 37 years, fell, mortally wounded. He would later die in Cork Regional Hospital, where he had been transferred from Ennis General Hospital. He was the first IRA man shot dead in the Republic since Tom Smith, who had been killed during an attempted jail break from Portlaoise prison in 1975.

With his partner fallen, the second raider made off on foot and hijacked an articulated truck which he drove to the quarry to reach the getaway car. The Ford was found the following day abandoned in the Maurice's Mills area of Clare.

The post office raiding party of just two that descended on Caher was unusually depleted in manpower for a subversive operation, but otherwise had many of the trappings of an IRA action. Besides the fact that the mortally wounded raider was a widely-known active service volunteer with the IRA, near the scene of the shooting Gardaí recovered an Armalite rifle, two revolvers, an air rifle, as well as balaclavas and two-way radios for monitoring police communications.

In the follow-up investigation, Kevin Walsh of Patrickswell was brought in for questioning. In custody, as on many other occasions, he fixed his concentration on a spot on the wall of the interrogation room and stayed mute until his release.

During the funeral oration, it was stated that Hugh Hehir was to have been on active service for the IRA when he was wounded. The oration was delivered by Coireall Mac Curtain from Broadford in county Limerick to a large funeral gathering that included the Sinn Féin publicity officer, Danny Morrison. With all the trappings of the paramilitary funerals that had become familiar in the North, with a tricolour-draped coffin bearing black beret and gloves, flanked by a republican guard of honour, Mac Curtain's oration stated that Hugh Hehir had 'died as a volunteer in the IRA'.

He described Hehir as a man of action and politics who believed the republican movement had the moral right, force and integrity to continue the struggle.

Virtually from the outbreak of the northern troubles, Hugh Hehir had been involved in republican activities and the armed struggle, initially in the North. In 1974 he had been arrested and later convicted on explosives charges for which he was sentenced to ten years in jail. While on remand in Crumlin Road Jail, Hehir was involved in an attempted escape. That failed jailbreak added a further 18 months to his sentence. Involved with him in the escape bid was Joe Doherty, the Belfast IRA man who would later figure in a long-running battle to avoid extradition from the United States. Hugh

Hehir was sent to Long Kesh. There, a fellow prisoner was Coireall Mac Curtain, who would deliver Hehir's funeral oration.

After his 1979 release from the Maze, Hugh Hehir resumed his IRA activity and was identified with a number of actions by the IRA in Munster where the unit which had its nerve centre around Patrickswell in county Limerick was primarily involved in fundraising armed raids. He and Kevin Walsh were linked to the armed robbery of a payroll for the giant Aughinish Alumina project in county Limerick. In that raid they overpowered and disarmed two Gardaí and locked them in the local Garda station. The Uzi machine guns taken from the escorting detectives later turned up in an IRA arms dump in England.

Hugh Hehir had also been linked to the elaborate fundraising kidnap by the IRA of the top-ranking executive of the then Quinnsworth/Crazy Prices supermarket multiple, Don Tidey. Abducted towards the end of 1983 by a heavily armed gang with some posing as Gardaí, he was freed after a massive three-week search by the security forces, but at a cost of two lives. During a comb-out in Derradda Wood close to Ballinamore in county Leitrim, a 22 year old Garda trainee recruit, Gary Sheehan, and 36 year old Irish Army sergeant and father of four, Patrick Kelly, were gunned down. During the fierce forest battle, a grenade was thrown and a Garda patrol car sprayed with bullets. With a party of three others from north Kerry, Hugh Hehir had been linked to the kidnap operation which reputedly was intended to take Tidey to Kerry, but a crash by the driver of a hired getaway car caused the switch to the area of fervent republican support in north Leitrim. The four managed to make their way back to home territory.

The oft-cited General Order 8 of the IRA rule book which states that it is 'strictly forbidden to take any military action against 26-county forces under any circumstances whatsoever' did not apply in Ballinamore, no more than it was to apply in Adare 13 years later.

Regularly trotted out to the media by the highly-tuned republican propaganda machine, the application of General Order 8 did not occur in other cases of cold blooded killing, two of which involved Gardaí.

In what was to all intents and purposes identical to the Adare raid and killing of Jerry McCabe, 27 year old Garda Frank Hand was shot dead while on security escort duty with a post office delivery van in Drumree, county Meath, in August 1984. Although they were armed with side guns and an Uzi sub-machine gun, the two Gardaí came under fire as they sat in their Fiat escort car watching the post office worker carry bags into the building. With a large haul of £220,000 involved, a gang of ten raiders took part in the operation. Two men armed with Sten sub-machine guns rushed from a garden beside the post office and opened fire. Garda Hand was hit in the chest and his colleague was slightly wounded. The money was subsequently recovered and convictions were secured in the Special Criminal Court, but it was indicated that the gunmen who fired the killer shots remained at large.

A member of the Fraud Squad, Garda Hand had married another member of the force just five weeks before and was one week back on duty after the honeymoon when he was shot dead. He was the 27th member of the Garda force to die violently since the foundation of the State, and the 11th since the 1970 outbreak of the northern troubles.

The killed in action list lengthened less than three months later, when unarmed Garda Sergeant Patrick Morrissey was brutally murdered when he gave chase after a post office robbery in Ardee, county Louth. Known throughout the Garda force and within the emergency and search and rescue services of the entire country as the former head of the Garda sub-aqua unit, he became involved when the getaway by two armed raiders turned into a débàcle. The raiders, who had earlier fired on a Garda car and crashed a getaway vehicle, were making off on a motorbike. They crashed through a Garda roadblock and hit a car injuring a woman driver and her three year old daughter. Sergeant Morrissey was felled as he gave chase. Immobilised by his wound, he was lying on the ground when one of the raiders returned and shot him in the face. Two men, one from Castleblaney in county Monaghan and the other from Crossmaglen in county Armagh, later received the longest sentences ever handed down in the Republic, Northern Ireland or Britain, when convicted of capital murder. Their death sentences were commuted to 40 years imprisonment.

Cold blooded killing, this time of an innocent civilian bystander with his young son looking on, had prompted a protest to government from the Association of Garda Sergeants and Inspectors about the rising level of bank robberies and other serious crimes of murder and kidnapping. Their call for action 'against ruthless and professional gangsters' came as far back as 1979. The appeal for urgent steps to be taken followed the shooting dead of civil servant, Eamon Ryan, during an armed hold up at a bank in his native Tramore in county Waterford. Then living in Leixlip in Kildare, he had returned with his family for a holiday after he had completed a Masters degree in Economics. He was a customer in the bank and accompanied by his son when four armed and masked men staged the robbery. Three unarmed Gardaí who arrived were held at gunpoint. During the raid, Eamon Ryan's child, oblivious to the danger from the gunmen, attempted to leave the premises. When the father moved to control the child, he was shot through the heart. Besides the public outrage which brought the leaders of the three main political parties in the Republic to Tramore to condemn the killing and comfort the Ryan family, the raid was worthless to the IRA and its war chest. Five days after the hold up, Gardaí recovered the £5,500 haul. Also recovered were an Armalite rifle and four handguns.

Chapter 8

The bike in the boot was the giveaway. When the alert went out that Gardaí had come under fire in Adare, the instinctive suspicions of Special Branch detectives were reinforced by the sighting of a bicycle in the boot of a car.

To the civilian, a bicycle jutting out of the boot of car would not merit a second glance. But in the town of Shannon it meant a great deal more. Particularly when the car with the bicycle on board was being driven by the partner of Gerry Roche. The woman driver, the car and the bicycle were very familiar to the particularly strong Garda contingent at Shannon. Detectives were especially familiar with that bicycle. They had trailed it often enough. That same bicycle had also been used to give them the slip.

Gerry Roche was just one of a substantial cast of republicans who lived in or frequented the new town of Shannon which had been described by Gardaí as 'the most policed town in the country'.

That was the observation made to *The Clare Champion* in the aftermath of the capture of Dominic McGlinchy, leader of the Irish National Liberation Army (INLA), and three accomplices after a ferocious night-time siege and shootout with Gardaí at a house near Newmarket-on-Fergus on St Patrick's Day, 1984. In that action, local armed detectives and an 18-strong task force unit from Dublin came under fire from an arsenal that included an armalite rifle, an Uzi machine gun and an American machine gun mounted on a tripod. The power of the gang's weaponry was demonstrated when bullets penetrated nine inches into cavity blocks that Gardaí were using for cover.

McGlinchy and his band of gunmen had won regular media headline notoriety as they rampaged through the Republic in a series of exploits more appropriate to bandits than freedom fighters. They had eluded capture and embarrassed security authorities to the point of mortification when capturing and stripping Gardaí of their uniforms which were to be used in further escapades.

Wanted in Northern Ireland for the murder of Toombridge postmistress, Mrs Hester McMallan, seven years earlier, McGlinchy was extradited to the North and handed over to the RUC at the border while his three accomplices were transferred from Ennis to the Special Criminal Court in Dublin. Charged with firearms offences were: 30 years old Ciaran Damery who gave his address as Kirkwood Villas in Cobh, county Cork; Seamus McShane of no fixed address but believed to be from Newry; and 28 year old Damien Bird with an address at Fatima Drive in Dundalk, county Louth.

Gardaí had been waiting for McGlinchy to surface in the Shannon area where he had placed his two sons in the care of local town councillor representing the Irish Republican and Socialist Party (IRSP), political wing of the INLA, Mrs Bridget Makowski. Mrs Makowski and McGlinchy both had Derry roots. He was from Belloghy and she had married her Polish husband in the United States, where she lived at the time, before returning to Ireland and settling in Shannon.

At the time of his capture, Dominic McGlinchy's sons, Declan and Dominic, were aged seven and five respectively. 'Of all the people in the Republic, Mrs Makowski was surely the wrong person to give the kids to. She is under surveillance all the time and there is more Garda activity in Shannon than any other part of the country,' a Garda remarked to *The Clare Champion*.

There were special reasons why Shannon was a hotbed of republican activity that came under incessant surveillance by the security forces. A substantial colony of people from Northern Ireland of republican or Catholic background had built up in Shannon due to the coincidence of events in Ireland and abroad. The town of Shannon was an urban development which had materialised out of nothing around the Shannon Industrial Estate and the concentration of overseas industry that had been attracted there since the 1960s. At the start of the troubles, refugees fled across the border from intimidation, hostility and physical force, and found refuge in a number of centres. At the same time Shannon was having troubles of its own because economic recession in the United States, home of most of its major firms, meant that jobs went from abundant to scarce. This had a knock-on effect on what had been dramatic growth in the new town. Shannon had entertained brighter hopes. At the time, the Shannon Development Agency, that included the town development in its remit, had drawn up plans based on forecasts of strong investment and jobs growth. On the strength of those predictions, the biggest housing scheme ever for Shannon had gone ahead.

So, when northern refugees came south, Shannon was the place where houses for rent were available and where there was also the promise of employment and a climate that supported entrepreneurial enterprise. While a predictable level of the northerners who came to Shannon availed of refugee supports, subsidised living and welfare, an appreciable number also proved to be a boon to the town and area through their industry and energy in building new lives and, in many cases, their own business ventures. As the northern contingent expanded, mostly in the same housing estate, figures with strong republican credentials and backgrounds also appeared in the town. As a result, the substantial Garda activity and numbers required in policing the Shannon Airport gateway for American flights was added to with round-the-clock anti-subversive duties for Special Branch detectives.

Gerry Roche was one of those who warranted ceaseless monitoring by the Special Branch. From Dun Laoghaire and affiliated to the INLA, detectives admit that he was one of the most difficult people to shadow and trail.

'He was constantly on the alert and most difficult to keep track of,' detectives of the era admit. 'Even when he was on the move he was always watching, always changing his route, or switching from one side of a street or road to the other. Always on the lookout and vigilant.'

He had reason to be vigilant. Identified with the assassinated Seamus Costello of the IRSP and its INLA military wing, Roche had a court conviction arising from a riot at the British Embassy, but had been subjected to more violent retribution in the cycles of internal feuding and blood letting that tore the INLA apart at regular intervals.

Whatever his reputation for caution and vigilance among the security forces, Roche certainly dropped his guard with almost fatal consequences when he was lured to a morning rendezvous outside Limerick in the first half of the 1980s.

He was waiting on the roadside when gunfire was directed at him from an approaching car. For Roche, the choice of meeting place worked in his favour and probably saved his life. For his attackers the chosen spot was all wrong because it was almost directly opposite the home of a detective. The detective's young daughter was sitting on the garden wall facing out into the road when the shooting broke out. Her father was having a Saturday lie-in, but immediately recognised the sound of the bullets flying outside his home. His first instinct was that he and his family were coming under attack. His hand gun was at his bedside and he was armed when he advanced out into the roadway. By that time the attackers had fled and their quarry was also out of sight. But the detective conducted a thorough search around the house and discovered Roche hiding in the undergrowth. He had not been hit by the gunfire but, in his panic, had fallen and suffered a deep gash in his leg. He was helped into the home of the detective where his wife cleaned up the wound. Although they could see that the gash had opened up almost to the bone, Roche adamantly refused to be taken to hospital, fearing that his attackers would track him down and corner him there.

Years later, in the cat and mouse game that Gerry Roche played with his Special Branch shadows, the bicycle was a cleverly conceived element of the tactics he employed to demonstrably outwit and frustrate the Special Branch men on his tail.

Detectives remember how Roche would take off on the bicycle or at other times move out of his Shannon base as a passenger in a car but with the bicycle in the boot. Once the bicycle appeared, the detectives knew exactly what to expect, but had to suffer the irritation of knowing that there was little they could do about it. Some time into his journey, Roche would switch from the car to the bicycle and take a route along a rural or suburban track or pathway that was inaccessible to the Garda car. While his trail would eventually be picked up again, detectives involved remember how Roche would often take a roundabout route through country laneways and paths simply to travel the 15 miles from Shannon to Limerick. But in shaking off the detectives and leaving them guessing as to his destination, Roche won time for a clandestine meeting or call.

Yet it was Gerry Roche's bicycle and old fashioned policing disciplines that alerted the Gardaí that something was happening. On the evening of Thursday, 6 June, a rank and file member of the Garda stationed in Shannon spotted the car driven by Gerry Roche's partner leaving the town and also noted that the infamous bicycle was jutting out of the boot of the vehicle.

As soon as the alarm was raised the following morning in Adare, Gardaí were immediately convinced that it was the work of the IRA active service unit operating from the Patrickswell area that Roche was associated with.

As the Special Criminal Court would hear in evidence more than two and a half years later, 'within hours' Gardaí were hot on the trail of known members of the Patrickswell gang and their associates. Raids and searches were legally authorised with houses and haunts checked out. Those raids in the immediate aftermath of the Adare shooting were carried out to establish where suspects were not, rather than where they actually were, to ensure that alibis of their whereabouts would not be contrived.

While IRA involvement was denied and the killers disowned by both the IRA and Sinn Féin, clear evidence that the abortive raid was the work of the IRA began to stack up rapidly, helped by the failures of the gang.

First there were the Kalashnikovs. The distinctively shaped weapons which had provided IRA fire power since the mid-1980s were recognised by Detective Ben O'Sullivan and civilian witnesses. Their correctness was corroborated by the cartridge cases strewn around the target vehicle. The ramming tactic was also familiar to Gardaí, as almost identical shock strategy had been employed two years earlier when the post office delivery vehicle had been rammed in a raid at Kilmallock in county Limerick. There too, a Kalashnikov had been used to fire on Gardaí.

But even more concrete evidence was left behind by the gang in their hasty retreat. Although containers of petrol, incendiary devices and other materials found in the jeep abandoned in Adare and the getaway car left in a forest, indicated that the plan had been to burn the vehicles, finds and forensic examination of both yielded valuable clues. Hair in a balaclava identified one of the raiders, and tracing the source of shotgun cartridges incriminated another. Careless overconfidence also exposed two others involved in the operation. They had neglected to take the precaution of wearing gloves like the gunmen, most probably on the presumption that the vehicles would be burned out. As a result, fingerprints were lifted from the vehicles of two men who were known to Gardaí. These men subsequently evaded capture.

The initial judgement by Gardaí that the deadly Adare operation was the work of the IRA group operating out of Patrickswell was rapidly confirmed. Cartridges found on the scene matched those collected after the armed raid at Kilmallock in 1994 which had been the work of the Provisional IRA. The finds also established that the shots had come from the same Kalashnikov rifle which had been fired at Gardaí in Kilmallock. Incendiary devices similar to the finds at Adare had also been recovered after the Kilmallock post office van ramming.

The hunt was on for known members of the IRA's Patrickswell 'fundraiser' unit. Authorised raids on homes and houses frequented by subversives took place in parallel with a roundup of prominent members of the republican movement and their associates, who were brought in for questioning.

From surveillance and intelligence work over the years, Gardaí believed that the unit of the IRA involved in the recurring fundraiser raids on vulnerable targets, such as post office cash deliveries, numbered around 25. But top Garda officers agreed that the subversives formed 'a committed hardcore meshed into a national network of support for the IRA, primarily hiding arms and transporting them to the North'.

While the top political strata in the region around Limerick that included three former Ministers for Justice – Desmond O'Malley, Gerard Collins and Michael Noonan – leaned towards a view that the level of republican paramilitary activity could have been more serious and widespread, there were times when the IRA men appeared to run riot. The extent to which the gunmen operated almost with impunity was played out on an April night in 1990 with the brief abduction of the Fine Gael Dáil Deputy of the time for the west Limerick constituency, Michael Finucane.

He was going about his routine cultivation of the local electoral grassroots when he stepped out of his car to attend a function at a venue in Croagh in county Limerick. In the darkness of the April night, he was confronted by a masked man carrying a gun. Two others then approached and he was bundled into a car. His head was pushed down as the car drove away. In the car he was recognised as a local member of the Dáil and, after a journey of some miles, he was ordered out of the car and told not to move. Once the car had gone, he made his way to the nearest town of Rathkeale.

The IRA would later telephone the Gardaí at the Askeaton district headquarters and asked that a message would be conveyed to 'apologise for any inconvenience caused to the Finucane family'. The IRA also contacted a local radio station to state that the deputy was unharmed. 'That may have been true, but only physically,' the Newcastle West politician confessed. He was a senator, and voicing opposition to any early release from prison of the Adare killers when he went public with details of his ordeal. He spoke in the Senate in 2004: 'Although it was over 14 years ago, there is an emotional scar,' he admitted.

In the 1996 Adare murder hunt, the earliest arrest was that of Patrick Sheehy, a married man and father of two who lived in Rathkeale but was a native of Newcastle West. His involvement with the republican movement had been on the records of the security forces since his 1981 court fine of £30 for an unauthorised collection during the H-Block hunger strike. He had later been fined for a 1985 assault and malicious damage, and had been sentenced to ten years in jail for his part in a post office robbery in Rathkeale. That sentence had been imposed in December 1989, seven years before the Adare post office robbery attempt would cost the life of a Garda.

Sheehy was held from 8 June, before being charged before the Special Criminal Court with membership of the IRA and possession of a firearm at Adare on 7 June with intent to endanger life.

On the same day, the carpenter and joiner, John Quinn from Faha in county Limerick, was also before the Special Criminal Court on charges of IRA membership and possession of ammunition on the eve of the Adare raid.

In less than two and a half weeks, the ever widening murder investigation had brought 23 people in for questioning, and a third man, Michael O'Neill, had been detained and charged with IRA membership before the Special Criminal Court. A forklift driver and father of nine children ranging in age from infant to early twenties, he had become acquainted with Jerry McCabe when the Garda was investigating the murder of O'Neill's sister by her own husband.

Thousands of statements were to be recorded, and up to a dozen taken in some individual cases, in an investigation that, at its peak, involved 300 Gardaí.

With three detained, the hunt was on for at least four more IRA men. Feedback from the Garda intelligence network indicated that two, if not three, had managed to decamp overseas and that one or two of the leaders of the Adare killer unit were being sheltered in IRA safe houses.

It would take 16 months before the fourth man, Pearse McCauley, was captured, and two months more before he was charged with having a direct part in the Adare crime. Totally in character with his legend within the republican movement and his flamboyant conduct in high profile court appearances, McCauley's capture was steeped in drama and menace.

From Fountain Street in Strabane on the dividing line between county Donegal at the uppermost tip of the Republic and his native county of Tyrone in Northern Ireland, McCauley all but flaunted his standing as a top member of the Provisional IRA who had figured on Britain's most wanted list in the opening years of the 1990s. Then he had established his links with Limerick when he was paired with the city's top IRA figure, Nessan Quinlivan, in IRA military action against the British mainland. They were captured in Britain and held, in November 1990, on charges of conspiracy to murder the prominent Conservative Party member, and one-time brewery chairman, Sir Charles Tidbury, and also with conspiracy to cause explosions. The pair were back in the headlines the following year when they made their way back to Ireland after a sensational armed jailbreak from Brixton Prison.

Spirited back to the Republic, McCauley returned to the headlines and the courts two years later when he was arrested in Dublin. He appeared before the Special Criminal Court on charges of possessing a pistol and ammunition for which he received a seven year prison sentence in November 1993.

He was nominated by the IRA for the early release conceded during what was variously described in the mid-1990s as a 'ceasefire' and 'cessation' of IRA violence, and termed a 'sos' or 'pause' within the IRA and most militant ranks of the republican movement. He was just two years into his prison term when he was released under the Department of Justice administration of Fine Gael Minister, Nora Owen.

On his release, McCauley had been immediately arrested to face an extradition warrant for his return to the UK to face charges there. He was granted bail and featured in both print and broadcast media, punching the air on his way out of the courts.

He was in the company of two men from Patrickswell and two from a border county when he was detained in Dublin in connection with a stolen car at the end of February 1996.

What it all added up to was that Pearse McCauley, on bail from the courts and just seven months out of prison on early release for republican prisoners, was part of the Adare operation where a detective was shot dead while seated defenseless and disoriented in a rammed car.

In May of the following year, an alert Garda spotted McCauley driving a car on the Belturbet to Ballyconnell road in Cavan. Gardaí followed him, but he took off at speed and briefly evaded the pursuers.

McCauley abandoned the car that had been identified and for which an alert went out, and called to the holiday home of an Englishman where he asked for a lift to the Slieve Russell Hotel.

Once they were in the Englishman's car, McCauley produced a gun and said, 'I think you have a problem.' He warned that if Gardaí caught up with them, his friends would shoot the man's family in England. Although McCauley threatened to shoot the man and to kneecap him, the man refused to budge and told McCauley he would take him no further.

The manhunt followed a trail across the country from Cavan to Sligo where the getaway car was found. Gardaí caught up with McCauley when he was cornered and arrested on a beach in Galway during a late night disagreement with his girlfriend in October. He was taken to Limerick where he refused to answer when asked to provide his name, address and date of birth by Detective Sergeant Christopher O'Brien at the Henry Street Garda headquarters, and nerve centre of the Adare murder investigation. McCauley was brought before the Special Criminal Court in December 1997 to be charged with capital murder and related offences.

In March of the following year, the Patrickswell IRA man on the top of the Garda most wanted list, Kevin Walsh, was flushed out in a major security operation around a farmhouse near Mullagh in Cavan.

Gardaí from Limerick involved in the hunt for those responsible for the shooting of their detective colleagues joined the action. They teamed up with Gardaí from the Cavan division and members of the armed Emergency Response Force when they surrounded the farmhouse of father of six, John Carolan, at Greagh na Darragh.

When the strong force of Gardaí rushed the house, they disturbed Kevin Walsh who was heavily disguised and had dyed his hair. He was armed to the teeth. In the back pocket of his trousers he had a Makarov pistol loaded with eight rounds of ammunition, and had a further eight rounds in a magazine in another pocket. In the bedroom used by Walsh, a fully loaded Kalashnikov assault rifle stood by the bed, ready for use. There were 60 rounds of ammunition in the weapon which was ready for semi-automatic firing with the safety lever off.

Altogether Gardaí seized a total of 136 rounds of ammunition, balaclavas, listening equipment to monitor Garda communications and a quantity of forged driver's licences and passports to conceal his identity and provide cover for escape overseas.

Captured on 10 March 1998, after 21 months on the run, the officer who charged Walsh after his capture was Detective Sergeant Dan Haugh from Henry Street Limerick headquarters. Walsh was initially charged under the Offences against the State Act. He was released just before midnight and then re-arrested by Detective Sergeant Haugh under section four of the Criminal Law Act of 1997 for the murder of Detective Garda Jerry McCabe.

On the following day, Friday, 12 March, Kevin Walsh was back in the Special Criminal Court where he had been sentenced to eight years in prison in the 1970s for his part in a Kerry bank robbery. Dressed in black sweatshirt and trousers, he did not stand and remained silent when eight charges were read out, including the capital murder of Detective Garda McCabe.

Chapter 9

300 witnesses had been mentioned, and the case was being estimated to go on for anything from three to six months, when the IRA gang was finally brought to trial more than two and a half years after the killing of Detective Jerry McCabe.

A total of 30 charges were brought against the five men from county Limerick who appeared in the dock of the Special Criminal Court at the Four Courts in Dublin on the opening day of the trial, Monday, 11 January 1999.

Four of the men faced a charge of capital murder which carried a mandatory sentence of 40 years imprisonment on conviction. They were Kevin Walsh (then 42) of Lisheen Park, Patrickswell, his neighbour Michael O'Neill (46), Pearse McCauley (34) from Strabane in county Tyrone but with no fixed address, and Jeremiah Sheehy (36) of Abbey Park, Rathkeale.

The four pleaded not guilty to the capital murder of Detective Garda Jerry McCabe and the attempted murder of his colleague, Detective Garda Ben O'Sullivan, at Adare, county Limerick, on 7 June 1996. They also pleaded not guilty to charges of possession of firearms with intent to endanger life, conspiracy to commit a robbery and possession of a quantity of assorted ammunition with intent to endanger life at Adare on the same date. They also denied unlawful possession of two rifles, a handgun and a shotgun with three shotgun cartridges at a farm located at Clonolea, Toomevara in north Tipperary, on the same date.

A fifth man, John Quinn (30) of Faha, Patrickswell, pleaded not guilty to unlawful possession of ammunition at Patrickswell on 6 June 1996, and conspiring with others between 5-8 June 1996 to commit a robbery in Adare.

When they appeared in the dock, the four accused of capital murder and related charges were dressed in dark grey suits and wore the green ribbon emblems of the campaign for release of republican prisoners.

The opening day of the trial was taken up with the charging of the five men and the broad presentation of the case by the counsel for the state, Mr Edward Comyn SC, who also outlined to the court the evidence and witnesses to be presented for the prosecution case.

Mr Comyn recalled for the court the events that took place in Adare on 7 June 1996, the number of shots that had been discharged and the three shots that hit Detective McCabe, one of which killed him almost instantly.

'Neither of the two Gardaí drew or used their firearms and it is the State's contention they never had any opportunity to do so,' Mr Comyn stated.

Besides the stolen Pajero jeep used in ramming the Garda escort car and the Lancer getaway vehicle, the State counsel said that a red Volkswagen van and a white Ford Transit van had also been used in the attempted robbery.

He detailed how ammunition and shotgun cartridges, a magazine for a Heckler and Koch assault rifle and a radio tuned to Garda frequencies had been among the finds in the Pajero. While a round of Kalashnikov ammunition was found in the Lancer car, none of the weapons used in the raid had been recovered.

In setting out the witnesses to be called, Mr Comyn said that one would identify Jeremiah Sheehy as the man seen driving the getaway vehicle after the shooting.

He said another witness would tell the court that a number of men arrived at his Patrickswell home in the Pajero and Lancer on the eve of the attempted robbery and had Kalashnikov rifles, a shotgun and a short firearm with them while they remained in the house until dawn. He said another witness would tell how five men arrived at his farm in Toomevara at nine o'clock on the morning of the aborted raid and said they wanted to stay at the farmhouse. They were armed with two military-style rifles, a shotgun and pistol.

Mr Comyn said the accused, John Quinn, was not at the scene of the shooting but had taken part in the preparation of the planned robbery.

The State counsel said Michael O'Neill was one of the men at the scene of the shooting in Adare and also at the houses in Patrickswell and Toomevara, while Jeremiah Sheehy's hair was found to match hairs found in a balaclava recovered at the scene.

Mr Comyn told the court that it was the State's case that Pearse McCauley was at the scene in Adare, and also at Patrickswell and Toomevara. Of Kevin Walsh, who had been arrested much later than the others, he said, 'it may be that he was the person most involved in the project in carrying out the enterprise that took place in Adare, but that would be a matter of inference.'

Walsh, the prosecutor added, had used his father's gun licence to buy a box of shotgun cartridges in Waterford in May 1996 and the cartridges were found in Adare.

Describing the killing of Detective McCabe as 'part of a well planned operation to rob the post office van', Mr Comyn said the evidence would show that the object of ramming the escort car and shooting the Gardaí was to immobilize the Gardaí and rob the van. The plan was to put the Gardaí out of action by close fire from an automatic weapon. 'The shooting was deliberate and at close range,' he said.

While the opening of the long-awaited trial for the capital murder by the IRA of a Garda commanded a dominant place in the broadcasting and print media, coverage moved onto the front pages a day later when Detective Ben O'Sullivan was the first witness called.

Standing in the witness box, Detective O'Sullivan bore physical evidence in his body that the judges and the court would not see. The right hand which he placed on the Bible to take the oath had one of its joints shot away. A knuckle on one of the fingers of his left hand had been wiped out. In the centre of one palm and in his right shoulder, fingers could have traced the bullet holes. Across his shoulder and back, the tracks of the bullets could also be physically felt, as well as the holes near his spine where the exit holes had been patched up and healed. He had spent 18 months under medical care. Ironically, the specialist treatment in repairing the gunshot wounds had been provided at Belfast City Hospital, where world-class expertise had been developed in responding to 30 years of mutilation by bomb and bullet. Surgery and treatment under specialist Barry Craig and his team in Belfast were followed by physiotherapy at Croom's orthopedic hospital outside Limerick city. His shoulder and back wounds would have been visible in countless hours in a hydropool and hundreds of lengths of swimming. His physically fit frame patched up, the psychological damage was also tackled in counselling sessions. He had returned to work in November 1997. 14 months later, across the courtroom in Dublin's Green Street, he was facing the men who had shot him and killed his colleague and friend.

The first element of drama occurred when the detective broke down in the witness box and the court had to pause while he composed himself. The breakdown occurred not while he was giving graphic first person details of the sudden burst of gunfire and the turmoil as thousands of steel particles exploded through their car. Instead, it happened as he was tracing the course of his career in the Garda force and came to the day, in 1972, when he moved out of uniform and into the plain clothes of the detective branch.

Asked by the prosecution counsel, Mr Paul O'Higgins SC, if he recalled if anyone else had joined the detective branch that day, he managed to say 'Jerry McCabe' before breaking down. He would break down several more times while giving evidence.

Having worked alongside his slain partner for 20 odd years, Detective O'Sullivan said their duties included dealing with subversives, escort and protection duty for high profile or high risk personages and VIPs, major crime investigations, escorting of cash in transit and bank protection.

He said he and Detective McCabe knew Kevin Walsh, Jeremiah Sheehy and Michael O'Neill, and knew Pearse McCauley and John Quinn by sight. Those men, he said, would also have known the two detectives, that they were Gardaí and that they were using an official patrol car in Adare on that morning of 7 June.

Of the shooting in which he suffered gunshot wounds that put him in an intensive care unit for four days, he recalled, 'it was automatic fire and there was silence between each blast.'

Driver of the post office truck, Willie Jackson, in his evidence said that he thought he was going to die and later thought that Detective O'Sullivan had died along with his partner.

He recalled how he had opened the door at the rear of the truck when he heard a bang and saw that a jeep had crashed into the back of the Garda car. He saw three men dressed in military-style fatigues and said they were armed with Kalashnikov rifles. He said the gunmen appeared to shoot into the patrol car. There were a number of bangs as he jumped down from the truck and moved to take cover in a door. 'I thought I was going to die,' he said.

When a silver car pulled up beside the truck, he thought he heard one man shout 'go, go' before the gunmen got into the car which sped off.

The truck driver tried to use his mobile phone to summon help but could not get a signal. He then went to the Garda car where he saw Garda McCabe with his head slumped on his chest. 'He appeared to be dead,' he said in evidence.

He also thought Detective O'Sullivan was dead and it was only when the seriously wounded and bleeding driver told him that he was using the wrong microphone for the Garda radio, that Jackson realised that the officer had survived the shooting.

The pandemonium, panic and horror that gripped Adare on the day of awful memory were reconstructed for the court by local witnesses.

The Adare postmistress, Miss Elizabeth Twomey, was dressing in her bedroom when she heard a bang followed almost immediately by shots. She looked out her window and saw a man with a balaclava at the driver's door of the Garda car. She also saw another man wearing a balaclava. She first made a 999 emergency call and then went to help Garda McCabe who appeared to be dead. She got towels and blankets to assist the shot Gardaí.

Living in Adare at the time, Gerry Hanrahan was driving a neighbour to the landmark Dunraven Arms hotel on the Limerick city side of the village when they heard a bang. He then saw a number of gunmen dressed in dark clothing and one of them appeared to be firing into a car. He drove on to the hotel and then went back up the Main Street. There a car pulled across the road, somebody threw him a mobile phone and said, 'Use it. They are killing guards up there.'

One of the staff at the Dunraven Arms hotel was Oliver Noone who had accommodation at what is known as 'the pink house' located on the same Main Street as the post office. He was woken by a bang followed by a loud noise like gunshots. He heard a voice say 'oh Jesus' as if someone was in distress or pain. Looking out the window he saw a man holding a weapon with a large magazine. The gunman was holding the weapon in a down position facing into the Garda patrol car. Behind the gunman, Noone saw the black Pajero jeep, its doors open and its wipers on. He told the Special Criminal Court that what he heard was 'quick, rapid fire'.

Shooting, shouting and moaning were heard from across the street by Mrs Terry Hogan. She had been woken by a bang and, going to the window of her house directly opposite the post office, she saw the delivery van and a man in a balaclava holding a weapon. She described it as 'a short, stubby gun'. She called to her husband who told her to get down and get away from the window. She then heard a lot of shouting and somebody moaning very loudly.

Having heard the pained, personal testimony of friend and partner Ben O'Sullivan when he described the storm of flying steel that devastated the inside of the Garda car and killed Jerry McCabe, Garda detective colleagues and officers sat through the clinical details of the injuries that caused the death.

In the everyday reporting of court proceedings, the conventions and protocols of the specialist aspect of news reporting has a traditional code of practice. In the interests of justice and fairness, the news reporting of court cases is largely confined to the facts and what is stated in evidence or otherwise in the protected privilege of the courtroom. But, in major cases in which there is the most widespread public interest, the press will regularly assign a 'colour' writer to describe the atmosphere and the human or 'people' aspects of the court procedures which, because of the weighty matters being adjudicated on, are normally ponderous, repetitive and very dry. The opening day of the Adare trial became what, in newspaper terminology, is called the 'marking' for the star descriptive writer at *The Irish Independent*. But the ensuing article prompted a court protest from the defence team representing the four who denied capital murder. The article which appeared under the headline *Smirking Quartet Put On A Loathsome Show* by the national newspaper's leading 'colour writer', Miriam Lord, whose impressions of unfolding major events were a fixture in the paper.

In place of the conventional manner of court reporting with straight unadorned and almost formal presentation of the facts, Miriam Lord put readers in the shoes of the members of the Garda force attending at the court and described the performance by the IRA men charged with capital murder. Just like the re-enactments from tribunal hearings for the Vincent Browne radio programme,

Miriam Lord's journalism brought the court proceedings to life. In place of detached recording of evidence, she painted word pictures.

Her article on the demeanor and conduct of the men in the dock who were facing the most serious charge that can be brought, told of men not only laughing and chatting through the proceedings, but of smirking, grinning and suppressed smiles as they acted out a show of bravado.

The protest on behalf of the four IRA men following the publication of the article was led by Mr Patrick McEntee SC, ranked among the top defence barristers in the land who commanded matching fees. Appearing for Pearse McCauley, he drew the attention of the judges to the article which he described as 'a highly emotive and pejorative attack' against the accused, and particularly his client, McCauley. He said McCauley regarded the article as calculated to damage the trial process.

Mr McEntee stated that McCauley had not indulged in any inappropriate conduct at the beginning of the trial and took the proceedings very seriously. He added that the article appeared to have the intention of prejudicing the readers of the newspaper, and the public in general, against the accused.

The comments from Mr McEntee were supported by the barristers representing Kevin Walsh, Jeremiah Sheehy and Michael O'Neill.

The presiding judge, Mr Justice Johnson, said that the court took notice of what had been said.

The pain for the McCabe family continued when Ben O'Sullivan's evidence on day two was followed the next day by the post mortem evidence of the Assistant State Pathologist, Dr Margaret Bolster.

She had been called to Adare on the day of the shooting where Detective McCabe's body was still in the patrol car seat at the preserved crime scene. She saw a pool of blood around the handbrake and bloodstains on the detective's trousers. There were holes in the back of his jacket and shirt. In his pockets she found a heavily bloodstained summons form, a pay slip, keys and a Garda Representative Association diary.

How medical assistance came to the scene promptly was also described in evidence to the court. Less than ten minutes after the cash in transit van had arrived in Adare, the call had gone out from the postmistress to Dr Nicholas Van Kuyk, a family doctor from the Netherlands who lived in Adare. His home was 300 yards from the scene of the shooting.

'I could see that the car had been badly shot up. The person in the passenger seat was slumped over and wasn't moving. I had been told by the postmistress that she thought he was dead,' he said.

The doctor carried out a quick examination of Detective O'Sullivan 'who was obviously in very bad pain but his vital functions were stable and he was not in immediate danger'.

He also carried out a quick examination of Detective McCabe. He opened the detective's shirt to listen to his chest but could find no heart action. He confirmed that the detective was dead and pronounced him so at 7.10 a.m.

During the examination, Dr Van Kuyk said he did not notice any wounds on Garda McCabe and the area of the detective's chest that he exposed for examination did not reveal any bullet entry or exit wounds.

It was a Garda colleague who had known Jerry McCabe for 27 years who identified the body. Sergeant Michael Gallagher, attached to Limerick's Henry Street headquarters, was called to Adare. He identified the body as that of Detective McCabe to the pathologist, Dr Bolster, at 2.07 p.m. – seven hours after the shooting.

The Garda forensic team that was rushed to Adare was headed by Sergeant Brendan McArdle of the ballistics section. He had been exercising in the Garda gymnasium when he heard the radio news bulletin of the Adare shooting and the death of a Garda and knew he would be heading to the scene as soon as a forensic team could be alerted.

Arriving at the crime scene, he conducted his initial searches around the body of Detective McCabe noting that his slain colleague was dressed in the old-fashioned style of a plain clothes detective, in jacket, shirt and tie, rather than the casual dress of the newer generation of detectives.

He also noted that Detective McCabe's handgun was still in his belt and the Sergeant took possession of the Uzi sub-machine gun which was still in the back of the car, still in its case, unloaded and with the safety catch on.

Around the Garda car, the forensics man found a large number of discharged ammunition of the type used in a Kalashnikov rifle. A further 58 rounds of similar ammunition were in a sports bag which was in the back of the Pajero ramming vehicle. That bag also contained 66 rounds of 9mm parabellum ammunition, 27 rounds of .22 ammunition and 18 shotgun cartridges.

Between the two front seats of the jeep he found a multi-band scanner which was programmed to a frequency that could quite clearly receive messages from the control room at Henry Street Garda headquarters in Limerick city.

A Kalashnikov assault rifle was produced for the court by Sergeant McArdle. He told the judges that the weapon was mostly found in 'places of insurrection' and said that the AK 47 and modified AKM models were the most frequently found in Ireland. He reminded the court that around 1,000 of the rifles had been spirited into the country in the gun running shipments of the mid 1980s.

He demonstrated to the three judges that the Kalashnikov had a selector lever which allowed shots to be fired either in semi-automatic or fully automatic mode. The rifle had a magazine holding 30 bullets, he said in evidence.

The ballistics expert said that when he tested the Kalashnikov in full automatic mode, it fired 15 rounds in 1.6 seconds. He had also carried out further tests. Even when wearing a heavy duty glove he had been able to fire seven short bursts of two rounds and one round. Even with the heavily gloved finger, he was able to control the rate of fire, he said.

Further forensic evidence was presented to the court on the fifth day of the hearing by Garda fingerprint expert, Detective Sergeant Christopher O'Brien. He told the court that the Pajero jeep used to ram the Garda car and the getaway Lancer car had been dismantled in an exhaustive search for fingerprints. He told the judges that no fingerprints had been found that belonged to the four men on trial for capital murder. But two other prints had been found in the Lancer. 'Those two people are still being sought in relation to this crime,' the judges were informed.

Starting into its second week, the trial took a totally new turn. In setting out the case in his opening address to the court, Senior Counsel Edward Comyn had told the judges that they would hear evidence from different witnesses about the movements of the defendants on the night before and day after the Adare action which had put them in the dock on charges of capital murder.

Those witnesses and their direct evidence were not forthcoming.

Patrick Harty, the bachelor farmer in his early fifties from the Toomevara area outside Nenagh in north Tipperary, who had made several statements to Gardaí about harbouring five men and concealing their weapons before collection, refused to take the oath and give evidence when he was called to the witness box. The judges committed him to jail overnight to rethink his position. But the Harty setback was only the start.

In quick succession, the sister and father of Kevin Walsh, who had been identified to the court in the opening of the case as the key figure in the Adare robbery operation and its consequences, suffered loss of memory. Both Sally Walsh and her father, Patrick, of Lurriga, Patrickswell, told the court that they could not remember events at their home on the eve of the shooting of the two detectives. They also said that they could not remember giving statements to investigating Gardaí and neither could they recall signing their signatures to the statements. The prosecution then asked the judges to treat both of the Walsh family members as 'hostile witnesses'.

For the prosecution, matters did not improve when the trial went into Tuesday of the second week.

The Toomevara farmer, Patrick Harty, was returned to the court and when he again refused to give evidence, and also refused to give reasons for his actions, he was sentenced to 18 months in jail for contempt of court.

On that seventh day of the case, the first of two 'trial within a trial' legal arguments took place.

Before the court had adjourned the previous day, Mr Comyn of the prosecution team had indicated that video evidence was to be presented to the court. It would be explained to the court that the video was a compilation of various Sinn Féin and republican gatherings, parades and commemorations. The footage had been put together by the Garda investigation team and used for identification checks with two witnesses who had been in Adare on the morning of the killing.

Witness Nicholas Bowden said in evidence that he had seen a man with ginger hair sitting on a wall at the Lantern Lodge outside Adare shortly after he saw five or six cars in convoy driving through the village around 5.30 in the morning, approximately 80 minutes before the Garda car came under fire. Detective Garda Nicholas Deenihan told the court that Mr Bowden had twice identified a man seen in the video scenes.

Another witness, Denis Bewick, told the court of having to brake hard when a silver car shot out of a junction in Adare on the morning of the killing. He said the driver of the car had a moustache and brownish hair. Replying to questions from the prosecution, he said he had picked out a man at least four times from the video he had been shown and had also picked out a picture from a photo album. However he added, 'But I can't say for sure whether it was the person I saw in the car or not.' He said he could not be 100 per cent sure if the man he picked out was the same man he saw driving the car on that morning in Adare.

The legal arguments and submissions to the court went on throughout the day and into the following day. Making a case why the identification based on the video compilations should not be allowed was the defence counsel for Kevin Walsh. Mr Anthony Sammon contended that the video introduced highly prejudicial material. He said that the video had been assembled after Kevin Walsh had been charged with capital murder. He also submitted that while Walsh had been asked to take part in an identity parade at the time of his arrest in March 1998, he had not been asked to do so before Gardaí showed the video to potential witnesses.

The legal disputation by the opposing teams ran into the next day and while the presiding judge made a ruling on the 'trial within a trial', the spectre of witness intimidation was brought into the public arena on the eighth day of the trial.

After completing his evidence about identifying the man with ginger hair that he had seen sitting on a wall in Adare on the morning of the shooting, witness Nicholas Bowden requested the permission of the court to ask a question. When his request was granted he said, 'I just want to know why should I be intimidated and threatened before I came to court?'

The presiding judge, Mr Justice Johnson, said that the witness was 'perfectly entitled to go to the Garda and make such complaints to them'. Mr Bowden did not elaborate on who or where the threats had come from.

On the issue of the video compilation that Mr Bowden and Mr Bewick had been shown, Mr Justice Johnson ruled that the video was admissible in evidence but qualified that by saying that the weight of the identifying evidence would be a matter for argument at a later stage in the trial. That later stage was not fated to come round.

The presiding judge said that having seen the video, the court was satisfied that it was 'fair regarding its content and variety of persons involved'. He added that there was a clear distinction between the admissibility of the evidence and the weight that would be given to the same evidence in coming to a conclusion.

It was in the closing stages of the eighth day of the trial that the Special Criminal Court heard the opening evidence regarding John Quinn, the fifth man charged before the court on lesser charges of conspiracy to rob. Over the following days, the circumstances in which Quinn was charged, detained and questioned would bring about a second 'trial within a trial' and ultimately lead to the abrupt termination of the case with an agreement to a reduced charge of manslaughter for the four who had faced capital murder charges.

From the ninth day of the case, and over two further days when the trial went into its third week, the court hearing was focused entirely on what happened when John Quinn was among the first to be detained in the murder hunt. A succession of Garda witnesses gave evidence of statements they had taken from Quinn while under interrogation at Henry Street Garda headquarters. Detectives involved in the interrogation and uniformed Gardaí involved in station duties gave evidence of how Quinn went into a state of collapse on a number of occasions and had to be taken to hospital. Throughout their evidence, Garda witnesses were challenged and pressed in cross examination by John Quinn's defence counsel. All suggestions of ill-treatment and intimidation towards Quinn were vigorously denied by Garda witnesses. Hospital and emergency staff also bore witness that at no time were injuries, or evidence of ill-treatment, apparent during examination of Quinn at Limerick Regional Hospital.

What the judges of the Special Criminal Court were being called on to decide in the 'trial within a trial', was whether to allow as evidence the statements that Gardaí said had been made by Quinn. But that too would not come to pass.

Chapter 10

'Mr Harty, from the book of evidence you have evidence to give of an extremely important nature.'

This observation on the seventh day of the trial was made by the presiding judge, Mr Justice Richard Johnson. The use of the words 'extremely important' could be interpreted as an indication that Patrick Harty and the statements he had given to investigating Gardaí were of high significance in the prosecution case.

Then 53 years old, Harty had given four statements to Gardaí about the movements of the five IRA men who had fled from Adare after the unmarked Garda car and its two occupants had been sprayed with automatic gunfire.

During the opening address to the three judges of the Special Criminal Court on behalf of the state prosecution, senior counsel, Mr Edward Comyn, had indicated that the state case would include a witness who would provide evidence of how the IRA men came to a farm in Toomevara, and stayed overnight. It was also indicated by the leader of the prosecution legal team that evidence would also be forthcoming about weapons which were left for collection at the farmhouse and instructions given for potentially incriminating clothing to be destroyed.

But on the sixth day of the trial, when Patrick Harty was called as a witness for the prosecution, he refused to take the oath and told the judges that he could not take part in the case.

He was then warned by the presiding judge that he had been summoned as a state witness and had a duty to give evidence. Otherwise, he would be in contempt of the court.

A brief adjournment was then called so that Harty could consult with his solicitor, but when he was again called to the witness box, he said in a low voice, 'I am very sorry, I can't.'

Having consulted the Director of Public Prosecutions about the development, Mr Comyn, said he had been instructed to seek a postponement of 24 hours before the court dealt with the matter.

Saying that Harty was 'under extreme stress', his solicitor also asked for more time.

The presiding judge held that Harty was in contempt of court and ordered that he be detained until the following morning when the court would deal with the issue.

It was his solicitor, Ms Liz MacGrath, who spoke for Harty when he was brought back to the Special Criminal Court on the following day. She told the judges that it was 'with deep regret' that the farmer was not in a position to purge his contempt. She added that he regretted that he was also unable to give a reason why he could not give evidence.

Declaring that the court was dealing with 'a crime of the utmost gravity', Mr Justice Johnson said, 'It is the duty of every citizen to give every assistance they can in a major criminal trial.'

Harty's refusal to give evidence despite legal advice left the court with no option but to impose a sentence of 18 months, the judge said. It was during his comments to Harty and his legal advisor that the judge pointed out that the evidence was 'of an extremely important nature'.

Later in that seventh day of the trial, the Special Criminal Court heard protests from a witness about intimidation.

Harty was to have a change of heart while he was held in Arbour Hill Prison. However, in the period that it took for him to decide to give evidence, circumstances had also changed in the court. There the State had also changed its stance and had decided that, in the circumstances, a plea of manslaughter would be accepted in place of the charges of capital murder against the four IRA men.

In the days when Harty was in the headlines as a central figure in the trial, his solicitor twice made statements and submissions to the court.

The solicitor, Ms Liz MacGrath, whose legal practice was located in Nenagh, had acted for Harty from the early 1980s. Having made four statements to Gardaí when he was implicated in the aftermath of the Adare shooting, in the lead up to the trial pressure had been put on Harty to change his solicitor. Ms MacGrath told the court, 'Being a religious man, he would not take that way out.'

When she entered the legal profession, Ms MacGrath was following in the footsteps of her father, the late Michael McGrath, who had served as the District Justice in the jurisdictions stretching across the midlands to county Carlow. The setting of the trial and its proceedings were also familiar to the solicitor as her late father had also sat as one of the three judges on the Special Criminal Court.

Speaking on behalf of her client during the trial, the solicitor said that Harty was carrying out his civic duty as a citizen of the Republic when he made his statements to the Gardaí.

In addition to the pressure to change his solicitor before the trial commenced, Ms MacGrath said she had reason to believe that further pressure was put on him.

Having previously informed the court that Harty was a bachelor who resided alone on a farm located in a 'secluded' spot and that he had no brothers and sisters, the solicitor would add later that the pressures on her client 'led him to fear for his safety and the safety of others'.

Harty had been unable to withstand the pressure any more, the solicitor said. His failure to carry out his civic duty played deeply on his mind and Ms MacGrath reported that he told her, 'Liz, I fell at Beecher's Brook.'

Describing her client as 'a decent, honest, loyal man who did not wish to give offence to anyone', the solicitor told the judges, 'the only reason he has found himself before this court is due to his obliging nature and sense of loyalty to the past which was clearly manipulated.'

On the 15th day of the trial, when the IRA men changed their pleas from not guilty to capital murder, to guilty of manslaughter, which was accepted by the state prosecution, Ms MacGrath applied for Harty to be released from prison. Then detained in Arbour Hill Prison for his contempt of court since 19 January, on 3 February his solicitor told the judges, 'Mr Harty is sitting in jail, not a happy man, and not just because of the term of imprisonment.'

Back on the milestone day six of the trial when Patrick Harty shocked the Special Criminal Court and the country by refusing to give evidence for the prosecution, two further witnesses subpoenaed to give evidence were declared 'hostile witnesses'.

They were the sister and father of Kevin Walsh, in whose house in Patrickswell the IRA men before the court and others stayed on the eve of the killing. Both Sally Walsh and Patrick Walsh repeatedly told the court that they could not recall the events of the night of 6 June 1996.

When summoned to the witness box, Sally Walsh stated that no one had called to her house on the night of 6 June, and that she did not remember seeing guns in the house.

Then Garda Inspector James Browne gave evidence of going to the Walsh house with Garda Dan Haugh and taking a statement from Sally Walsh.

But when Ms Walsh was recalled to the stand she told the prosecuting state counsel, Edward Comyn, that while she knew Inspector Browne, she could not recall making a statement to him.

Asked about her attitude to the killing of Detective McCabe, she said, 'My personal feeling is that nobody has the right to take a life.'

She said she had never refused to help the Gardaí investigating the McCabe murder. She added, 'Some people say I live in my own world. I have been threatened. I have been very ill for the past few years and I can't recall if I did say anything.'

Saying that she did not know why she was in court, Sally Walsh contended that she should not be there. She said that she had been threatened when she was seeing the Gardaí, that they had told her she would be shoved down the stairs and they would let people into the cell to rape her.

Patrick Walsh was declared a hostile witness after he told the court that he could not recall making a written statement to Gardaí, or making a sketch for them showing the position of vehicles in his yard on the eve of the Adare shooting.

Inspector Browne said he had written down a statement made by the witness when he was in custody in Henry Street Garda station on suspicion of IRA membership.

The Inspector said that Patrick Walsh had told him he was upset over the events in Adare and he wanted to make a statement. Inspector Browne said that Mr Walsh had corrected the statement after it was written down, and had then signed it.

When Patrick Walsh was also recalled to the witness box and shown the statement, he denied that it was his signature. 'My memory is not great,' he said.

What would later be cited as the turning point in the trial that convinced the state prosecution to accept a lesser plea than capital murder, was followed by other difficulties.

Over the subsequent days, what was described as 'a trial within a trial' took place. At issue were the statements made to Gardaí by John Quinn, who had been described as an 'associate' of the IRA gang based in Patrickswell and was described to the court as a 'messenger' or 'go-for' by the senior Garda officer who had led the Adare capital murder investigation.

For four days, the defence barrister for Quinn, the Queen's Counsel, Ms Eilis McDermott, challenged the admissibility of all the statements, both verbal and oral, that Quinn had made when in custody. In cross-examination of witnesses, Ms McDermott raised questions of ill treatment of Quinn, while the court heard evidence of how he had been taken to hospital on four occasions but each time had been returned to custody in the Garda headquarters in Limerick.

John Quinn had been among the first suspects to be arrested and charged in the early days of the Adare killing manhunt. The court was told by Detective Sergeant John Heelan that he had spoken to the defendant on the day after the murder. When questioned about his movements the previous night, Quinn had stated that he had gone to Limerick for a pint and then returned to Patrickswell.

But the detective sergeant traced a security video that showed Quinn at a petrol filling station on Limerick's Dock Road at 1.05 a.m. The Garda witness said he had arrested Quinn on Sunday, 9 June. Quinn was detained under Section 30 of the Offences against the State Act as the detective was of the opinion that Quinn had information relating to the possession of firearms in Adare on the day of the shooting.

On his first night in custody, Quinn had been questioned at Henry Street Garda headquarters by three Gardaí. The senior officer was Inspector John Courtney. With him were Sergeant Tom O'Brien and Detective Garda Pat Kelly.

Inspector Courtney said in evidence that Quinn had asked about Jerry McCabe's family and added, 'I am an innocent man. I didn't shoot anybody.'

Quinn, according to the testimony of Inspector Courtney, told the Gardaí that he had a problem with his back arising from a traffic accident three years previously and sometimes his spinal disc would 'go out'. While being questioned, Quinn had complained about his back, lay on the floor and pretended to lose consciousness.

'He just slid down onto his knees and onto the floor and pretended to faint. He was there for a minute or two,' said Inspector Courtney.

Having decided that Quinn was 'feigning', the Inspector and the other Gardaí lifted him up and put him back on the chair. 'We lifted him bodily off the floor, the three of us. He started to grin at us and smirk. He was trying to frustrate the investigation. That's why I had him lifted off the floor and put back on the chair.'

Inspector Courtney added that Quinn refused to answer any questions about his movements or about subversives he might have known. He said he was not involved in the murder and was sorry for the dead Garda's wife and family, but he had nothing to do with it.

The Inspector said that Quinn then flung himself on the floor, lay down on his back, grabbed the leg of a table and a door stop and lay stretched out on the ground. 'At that stage I knew he was only acting up,' the Inspector told the court.

Quinn continued to lie on the floor while the Gardaí went outside the interrogation room to a corridor where the Inspector said he wrote up a record of the interview. When asked to sign the note, Quinn replied, 'Fuck off.'

Under cross-examination by Ms McDermott QC, Inspector Courtney agreed that there had been 'enormous grief' at the murder of Detective McCabe. When she asked if there was also anger, the Inspector replied, 'Naturally.'

While conceding that he had no medical training, Inspector Courtney said that he was dealing with 'a fit, active, hardy young man who worked on a building site'. In his opinion, Quinn was feigning.

The Inspector agreed that Quinn was later examined by a doctor and stated that he was 'delighted' when Quinn was taken to hospital. 'We could get nowhere with him. It was a lost cause. The thing was a farce,' he added.

The Inspector denied that he had assaulted Quinn or that any other Gardaí had assaulted him. He also denied that he saw injuries to Quinn's mouth, jaw, neck, arms and hands, stating that he had no injuries whatsoever.

Inspector Courtney also denied the suggestion from the defence counsel that the custody regulations did not apply to him and that he was only interested in getting information. He further denied that the strategy adopted by Gardaí was to physically ill treat Quinn to get him to talk.

Detective Garda Patrick Kelly, who had been called in from his Clonmel base to assist the Adare investigation led by Inspector John Kerin, said he knew John Quinn as 'a close associate of members of the gang'. He acknowledged that when Quinn was interviewed, Gardaí had no evidence against him other than 'suspicion and belief'. But he denied that there was a plan by Gardaí to get Quinn to make incriminating statements. Under cross-examination by Ms McDermott, he denied any suggestion of ill treatment saying, 'Neither I nor my colleagues ever touched him. I certainly would not have compromised the most serious investigation I have ever taken part in by touching him.'

Garda Sergeant Dermot Gaffney, who was the member in charge on 9 June 1996 at Henry Street headquarters where Quinn was being detained, told the Special Criminal Court how Quinn's parents had called to the station to see their son and were accompanied by the family doctor. The defendant was examined by the doctor who requested an ambulance.

Over the following days, medical and Garda witnesses gave evidence about the four occasions on which Quinn had been taken to Limerick Regional Hospital.

Member of the ambulance crew that attended at the Garda headquarters on 12 June, Sally Duggan, said Quinn was conscious in the ambulance but did not communicate with any of the crew. She said she saw no reasons for any 'traumatic injuries'. In her evidence she also said she had noticed a bloodstain on Quinn's lip when he was in the cells area, but in the ambulance it had gone.

Press photographer Kieran Clancy, who was on the Limerick staff of *The Examiner* newspaper, said he took photographs of Quinn being taken from the Garda station, as well as entering and leaving the regional hospital on 12 June. The photographer said that Quinn appeared 'passive at all times' but did look directly at the camera once.

Detective Garda Arthur Ryan gave evidence of Quinn being taken to hospital on 11 June. When the doctor who carried out the examination said that he was discharging him, Quinn refused to get off the hospital trolley. The detective said that he and Garda Paul Madden lifted Quinn off the trolley and into a patrol car. On their return to Henry Street, Quinn again refused to get out and had to be lifted and brought to the cell area.

Further evidence of Quinn's behaviour in the Garda station and in movements in and out of hospital was given by other Gardaí. Sergeant John Kelly described how Quinn was 'shivering, shaking and gasping for breath' when he was taken from the Henry Street headquarters to an ambulance. The sergeant recalled seeing the ambulance crew fit an oxygen mask to Quinn, but when the ambulance arrived at the hospital, Quinn's difficulties appeared to have ceased. When Quinn was returned to the Garda station, he walked in unassisted and without difficulty. Detective Garda Padraig Clark gave evidence of seeing Quinn when he was brought back from hospital on 12 June. He was present when Quinn had been discharged and was being taken out of the hospital in a wheelchair. On the approach to the front door, he saw Quinn chewing something. With a number of press photographers waiting outside the entrance, Quinn then spat out a small amount of blood and saliva.

On 12 June, when Quinn was scheduled to be taken to the Special Criminal Court to be charged, he was again taken to hospital. In evidence to the 1999 trial, a consultant doctor said that, apart from slight tenderness to the sternum and upper abdomen, he could find no evidence of bruising, swelling or injuries.

Mr Ronan O'Leary who was head of the Accident and Emergency Department said he had examined Quinn to see if he was fit to travel to Dublin. The consultant said that Quinn was 'passively unco-operative' during the 15–20 minute examination and was 'voluntarily mute'.

The consultant said x-rays of Quinn showed no physical trauma and that no life threatening injuries were visible.

Gardaí gave evidence of interviews with Quinn in the period after his arrest on 9 June, two days after the Adare killing.

Detective Garda Padraig Clark interviewed Quinn on 10 June. The detective said that in this interview Quinn gave details of his involvement in the preparations for the planned Adare robbery, which he carried out on the instructions of Kevin Walsh up to the hours before the shooting.

According to the detective's notes of the interview, Quinn had offered to make a verbal statement 'off the record'. He later said, 'I'm a dead man. I'm looking at 30 years, ye know that. What if this got sanctioned from above? Where do I stand? I know it got the nod from above. I was told I'd be found in South Armagh with a bag over my head.'

Detective Clark said that Quinn repeatedly stated during the interview, 'I'm fucked. I'm a dead man.'

Under cross-examination from Quinn's defence counsel, Ms McDermott QC, the detective said he could see that a weight of guilt was on Quinn's shoulders. 'The murder of Detective Garda Jerry McCabe was weighing very heavy on his mind. I could see that he wanted to get it off his chest and talk about it,' the detective stated.

Detective Garda Gerard Dillon gave evidence of interviewing Quinn on 11 June. Although Quinn was afraid for his own safety and feared that he would be shot, he said he would make a statement about his involvement.

According to the detective's evidence of the interview, Quinn said that he had been involved in the IRA for a couple of years. He said Kevin Walsh was an IRA man who was known as 'The Fox' and described how Walsh had given him instructions from two weeks before the armed robbery attempt, up to the movement of a bag of weapons and the stolen vehicles into the Patrickswell area on the night before the Adare attack.

Cross-examined on behalf of Quinn, Detective Dillon said he did not injure Quinn and said nobody touched Quinn while he was present.

The defendant's complaints of ill treatment were raised when he was brought before the Special Criminal Court on Wednesday, 12 June. He had to be helped to his seat for the 20 minute hearing and when the charges were being read out, Mr Justice Freddie Morris directed that Quinn could sit down.

Quinn's barrister at that hearing was Mary Ellen Ring. She told the court that she had received instructions that, while in custody in Henry Street Garda station, Quinn had received a number of injuries.

The barrister stated, 'His present physical and mental condition is of concern. He had complained of periods of unconsciousness and memory loss as a result of injuries.'

Although evidence was given that Quinn had been taken to Limerick Regional Hospital for examination and that he had been discharged as fit to travel, Ms Ring said that Quinn had injuries to his face and body including swelling of the elbows and hands. She said he had also passed blood in his urine and had been unable to eat or sleep for 48 hours.

The barrister applied to the court to order that Quinn be sent to the Mater Hospital for a full medical examination. But Mr Justice Morris said there was no evidence before the court that Quinn was not fit to travel. Charged under the Offences against the State Act with membership of the IRA and possession of ammunition on the eve of the Adare killing, Quinn was remanded in custody to Portlaoise Prison.

While the trial came to a sudden end before the judges ruled on whether the statements said by Garda witnesses to have been made by Quinn would be admitted into evidence, the suggestion of ill treatment of Quinn during questioning was dealt with in a Dáil statement by the Minister for Justice.

In the course of the 9 February special debate on the Adare trial and its outcome, Minister John O'Donoghue responded at some length when the Sinn Féin Deputy, Caoimhghin Ó Caoláin, called for a full and open independent inquiry into allegations of ill-treatment.

The Minister did not present his own views to the Dáil but, instead, read into the record of the Dáil the comments made by Mr Justice Johnson, the presiding judge, during his sentencing of the Adare gang.

The judge's statement said:

In the course of the last three weeks many insinuations have been made against the Guards in the course of a long and detailed cross-examination on behalf of Mr Quinn. It should be pointed out that in the course of his detention, Mr Quinn visited hospital on no less than four occasions and was examined by no fewer than four doctors before he came to Dublin and was in the presence of numerous ambulance men and other medical auxiliaries. At no stage did he make any complaint to any one of them regarding his treatment by the Gardaí.

The court is satisfied, having heard the evidence, that Mr Quinn was treated whilst in custody strictly in accordance with the law and with the utmost professionalism, despite the fact that at the particular time the Gardaí must have been under immense pressure. The court was particularly unimpressed with the photographs taken of the accused leaving the hospital in Limerick and rejects absolutely the implications which it was intended that the court should take therefrom.

The Guards in our view, as stated, acted with patience and professionalism during the questioning and detention of Mr Quinn.

On the basis of the judge's remarks, the Minister for Justice told the Dáil that it was clearly the view of the court that there was no ill-treatment in the case.

The Minister added that Quinn had made a formal complaint to the Garda Complaints Board, alleging abuse of their authority by the Gardaí as well as the use of force and violence. 'These are, of course, being investigated by the Board.'

The Minister also told the Dáil of a second complaint of ill-treatment that had emerged from the Adare case from one of the four who had been charged with capital murder and pleaded to manslaughter.

'Upon his arrival at Portlaoise prison, Jeremiah Sheehy alleged that he had been ill-treated by the Gardaí,' the Minister told Deputy Ó Caoláin and the other members of the Dáil.

Sheehy had then been referred to hospital for medical examination, the Minister said and added, 'his allegations were investigated by a senior Garda officer who found that there was no ill-treatment of Mr Sheehy.'

Making the point that Sheehy had not made any complaint to the Garda Complaints Board, the Minister said, 'Allegations have been made generally about ill-treatment by the Gardaí of those who were sentenced. I have now expressed what the position is and I sincerely hope that what I have had to say will lay to rest, once and for all, uninformed comments regarding this matter.'

A brother of John Quinn, who refused to account for his movements on the day of the Adare shooting, subsequently won damages and legal expenses in a compensation claim against the State. Paul Quinn, also of Faha, Patrickswell, was 22 when he was arrested in July 1996 on suspicion of being a member of the IRA. He was later sentenced to six months in prison at Limerick District Court for failing to account for his movements on the eve and day of the killing of Detective McCabe. In a December 2000 judgement, which became final in March 2001, the European Court of Human Rights ordered that he be paid £4,000 compensation and awarded him legal costs of £11,341 for violation of his right to silence and privilege against self-incrimination.

Chapter 11

The extent of witness intimidation which emerged into public view in and around the Adare trial provoked an outcry, but it was nothing new to the security authorities of the State.

From the first Garda killing that followed the outbreak of the northern conflict, intimidation was a reality, according to the most senior security sources. Witness intimidation was the least of it. It was due to intimidation of juries that the no-jury Special Criminal Court was introduced in 1972.

That first killing was in January 1970 when Garda Richard Fallon was shot in the head while giving chase after a Dublin bank robbery by the republican splinter group, Saor Éire. A jury brought in a verdict of not guilty on the man charged with the capital murder who had been extradited from England to face trial. Even then, when the shooting dead of a Garda was a sensation that shocked the country, the security authorities entertained the most serious fears about intimidation in that trial. This has been confirmed from sources most closely involved in decision making by the government of the time. That government hoped the suspect would be put on trial in Britain for offences there. The view then was that there was a far greater chance that he would be convicted and imprisoned in Britain, rather than if he stood trial in Dublin.

Almost 30 years later, with the Special Criminal Court enduring for many years longer than had been anticipated initially, external interference still continued to stifle the administration of justice.

The intimidation that came to light in the McCabe trial had been orchestrated either anonymously or with such chilling menace that those responsible could be confident of keeping their identities hidden. But while surreptitious threats to witnesses were being made, a parallel campaign was taking place in the public domain. In what in other times and political circumstances would have been regarded and urgently dealt with as attempts to influence the process of the law, Sinn Féin figures at various levels were making public statements that floated excuses and explanations for the Adare killing. They also contended that those involved would qualify for early release if they were convicted. Beside the fact that the explanations and excuses were coming from quarters other than the Provisionals, there were further highly unusual, if not unprecedented, aspects to the campaign.

In January 1998, Martin Ferris, an IRA activist since the 1970s who had served a number of jail terms including a sentence for his lead role in the *Marita Anne* gun-running, came to Limerick from his neighbouring native county Kerry where he was an elected county councillor.

He was then a member of the Ard Comhairle of Sinn Féin and had previously been identified as a high ranking member of the Provisional IRA. At that time he was being groomed for the Dáil seat he would win in 2002 and, in the candidate cultivation culture of Sinn Féin, had moved into the limelight of political respectability surrounding the party leadership. He had been included in a party delegation meeting with the British Prime Minister, Tony Blair, a short time before.

He came to Limerick ostensibly to speak at the annual commemoration of Sean South, the celebrated-in-song casualty of the 1950s IRA border campaign. The visit also served a double purpose, as it coincided with the campaign of a Sinn Féin candidate in a by-election to fill the Limerick East Dáil seat of the deceased socialist, and staunch opponent of the IRA, Jim Kemmy.

In relation to the killing of Detective McCabe, in the fundraising raid for which the IRA had accepted that those involved were its members, Martin Ferris said, 'the tragic death of Detective Garda McCabe certainly did not help the republican struggle. It should not have happened but unfortunately, and accidentally, it did happen.'

So how did Martin Ferris come to the knowledge that the shooting had been accidental? His remarks were made in January 1998, two months before Kevin Walsh was finally captured in a raid on a remote farmhouse in Cavan.

How did it come about that, while the person identified by Gardaí as the prime suspect in a capital murder investigation was still on the run, Councillor Martin Ferris could publicly state that the snuffing out of the life of a Garda Detective in Adare had happened 'accidentally'?

And why was it that nobody, including the media and those charged with enforcing the law of the land, pressed Martin Ferris for answers on how he could state, with such certainty, in public, that the killing had occurred 'accidentally'?

Just three months later, on 14 April, the security correspondent with *The Examiner*, Brian Carroll, reported that Martin Ferris had issued an ultimatum demanding the release of all political prisoners, including those involved in the killing of Jerry McCabe.

Yet again, Sinn Féin would refute the report, but a matter of weeks later it had changed its position. This time it was Donal Cusack, a fellow member with Councillor Ferris of Sinn Féin in Kerry, who went public with the reiterated demand.

Cusack demanded, 'We must see the release of all political prisoners,' but with the concession, 'We understand this is an emotional question, especially for the family of Jerry McCabe. But we believe the people who were involved were politically motivated.'

'The killing of Jerry McCabe was wrong. It should never have happened. But those awaiting trial should be regarded as political prisoners and should be released,' he added.

That intimidation of witnesses was anticipated by Gardaí and state authorities prosecuting the Adare capital murder case, also became clear in legal steps taken during 1998.

In March of that year, the senior counsel prosecuting the case, Edward Comyn, asked for, and received, the consent of the Special Criminal Court in witholding 32 documents from the legal teams acting for the accused.

The court was told that the documents were sensitive and that it would not be in the public interest for the documents to be released to the defence.

Further evidence of anxiety about the possibility of intimidation of those involved in the case emerged almost on the eve of the trial.

In the early part of December 1998, Mr Comyn again appeared before the judges of the Special Criminal Court seeking exemption. This time he asked that four statements from Garda informants not be made available to the defence.

In that application, a sworn affidavit from Limerick's Garda Chief Superintendent, Michael Fitzgerald, was read to the court.

While saying that the statements were not relevant to the defence of the five men facing the charges, the Chief Superintendent's affidavit added that there was a 'real and serious risk of injury if identities were disclosed'.

The three judges read the four statements that the state did not want disclosed to the defence. Mr Justice Richard Johnson, presiding, said that the court would keep the documents under review during the trial.

In the course of the subsequent trial, one witness spoke out against threats made against him when protesting to the court. The judges also heard of other threats to the safety of a witness which were elaborated on in statements from Gardaí and TDs when the trial came to a premature conclusion, with intimidation cited as the decisive factor.

In the special Dáil debate on the Tuesday after the Adare trial came to a unexpectedly early end, the issue of intimidation was dealt with by the Minister for Justice and by members of the opposition.

The Labour Party Deputy Brendan Howlin pointed out that in the aftermath of the trial, newspapers had reported that the Gardaí were satisfied that six witnesses were victims of intimidation. He added that one of the witnesses had been threatened that his house would be burned down if he gave evidence in the case.

He asked why the government had allowed a situation to develop in which witnesses with crucial evidence, in a case involving the most serious charge that can be laid, that of capital murder, 'were left to the mercy of thuggish elements whose commitment is to intimidation and not to justice'.

Accusing the republican movement of 'hypocrisy', Deputy Howlin told the Dáil:

> *They are prepared to resort to the courts when it suits them, yet those associated with the republican movement are willing to resort to the vile practice of threats and intimidation to pervert the course of justice and prevent members of their organisation from being held to account in the way that the vast majority of the citizens want and expect.*

But while the courtroom protest of one witness who had been subjected to threats brought witness intimidation into the public view, there were other sides of the issue to look at.

During the Dáil debate on the McCabe case, Minister for Justice, John O'Donoghue, made it plain that it was not simply a matter of protecting witnesses, but also a question of what sort of protection the witnesses would accept.

In the McCabe case, the Minister acknowledged that 'the protection of witnesses was an issue'.

In taking up the matter during his lengthy statement, the Minister relayed to the Dáil what had been reported to him by the Garda authorities. While telling the Dáil that he accepted that 'witnesses may have been intimidated in this case', the Minister added that the level of police protection provided was determined not by the Gardaí but by what the witnesses themselves would permit. 'What the witnesses accepted was the maximum in terms of security arrangements they could be prevailed upon to accept,' the Dáil was informed.

'Protection was offered and certain protections were given,' the Minister revealed, but would not go into details. He acknowledged that two witnesses who had identified key figures in the crime had reported intimidation to the Gardaí. But again the Minister added that while protection was offered, 'they did accept a certain level of protection which the Gardaí were very pleased to tender.'

The leader of the opposition, John Bruton, and his Fine Gael party spokesman on justice, Jim Higgins, joined with Brendan Howlin in raging against the intimidation during their Dáil debate contributions.

Deputy Bruton, who had been Taoiseach at the time of the Adare shooting, had harsh words for the IRA and its methods. 'Given the well known ability of the IRA to hold entire communities in nationalist areas of Northern Ireland under their particularly vicious form of policing, it was surely entirely predictable that intimidation of witnesses would be a feature of this case,' he contended. Knowing the IRA's record, 'the question of witness intimidation should have been dealt with before the case opened,' he said.

The 'clear evidence of blatant intimidation' was cited alongside other factors by the Fine Gael justice spokesman, Deputy Higgins, in a strenuous attack on the State's decision to accept the manslaughter plea, which he described as 'hoisting the white flag'.

Declaring that the compromise sent out all the wrong signals, he returned to the issue of witness intimidation. 'It is a clear indication that intimidation rules,' he stated. 'It underlines the manner in which intimidation can compromise the principles of democracy. It undermines the judicial system and subverts law and order.'

Yet a different perspective on the tactics and consequences of intimidation came from the Fine Gael benches, and from a Deputy who had first hand experience of the terror inspired by subversives.

Deputy Michael Finucane had been briefly abducted by masked men who probably were part of, or associated with, the IRA group operating in the area of west Limerick where he was born, worked and lived.

Having heard the Minister mention during the debate that the Garda Commissioner had assigned a superintendent in the force to investigate the intimidation of witnesses in the case, Deputy Finucane delivered prophetic observations and incisive questions.

Saying that the level of intimidation involved in the case had 'obviously influenced the change of charge', he posed the question, 'Does the Minister honestly and sincerely expect that people who have been intimidated, even if they knew the names of individuals, will wreak further intimidation on themselves by revealing them?'

Similar sentiments were expressed by a onetime senior figure in the security establishment who has since retired. In relation to the follow-up investigation into the intimidation of witnesses, he pointed out, 'In most cases, those who have been intimidated do not make it known. In cases of intimidation where complaints are lodged, it is absolutely understandable that those who were subject to intimidation would be most reluctant to put themselves at further risk by co-operating with an investigation.'

Hopes were much higher at the end of the Adare trial when the Garda who led the investigation provided details of how the intimidation was applied. Then Detective Inspector John Kerin said, 'At least three vital civilian witnesses were threatened and intimidated.' In two cases the threats had been made over the phone, but in the third case IRA people called to the home of the witness and 'told him not to give evidence'. The Inspector added, 'We know that a number of leading IRA men in the Munster area called on him.'

Even before the Minister for Justice, John O'Donoghue, announced to the Dáil that the Garda Commissioner had appointed a senior officer to investigate the intimidation, Inspector Kerin stated that an investigation was taking place. 'I am satisfied that arrests will be made,' he said.

The investigation was entrusted by the Garda Commissioner to then Superintendent KT McGann of the Anglesea Street regional Garda headquarters in Cork. The outcome of that investigation was that 'no evidence of criminality was discovered to warrant the investigation file being forwarded to the Director of Public Prosecutions', the Garda Press Office confirmed.

Chapter 12

'Plea bargaining' would have been best known to the Irish public through fictional courtroom scenes seen on television and cinema screens. At its simplest, plea bargaining was seen to boil down to a trade off between the prosecution and defence sides. The bargain could be negotiated for a multitude of reasons. In the American system, plea bargaining can serve as a shortcut that frees up the courts by substantially reducing time spent in hearings. In other instances, bargains can be reached in which lesser charges with lesser sentences are pressed in return for co-operation in other criminal investigations. The purposes for which plea bargaining is entered into can also include arrangements that are mutually agreed when developments in a court hearing are not going to plan, or in cases where one side or the other wants to save a person or information from exposure to the public.

While questions about plea bargaining in Irish courts had arisen in the past, most notably in the Malcolm McArthur case, it was the Adare trial which unleashed a torrent of critical public comment and brought the plea bargaining process into high profile. In the McArthur case, political controversy was piled on sensation in a double murder investigation. There was an astounding climax to the hunt for the murder suspect, Malcolm McArthur, when he was discovered in the apartment residence of the Attorney General of the time, who subsequently resigned. McArthur went on trial for one murder but the decision by the State not to bring the second murder to trial provoked protest from the family of the murdered man and widespread media speculation that an arrangement had been negotiated for McArthur only to be tried on one charge.

As was starkly demonstrated in the subsequent outcry, that a plea bargain might be arrived at in the McCabe case was most unexpected outside the precincts of the Special Criminal Court and the legal fraternity. But it does happen. And when it happened, it came as a surprise to the Taoiseach, his Minister for Justice and to the Dáil legislature. It was not only a surprise, but a bolt from the blue to the widow and family of the slain detective.

It would be described as showing the white flag and surrender in the privileged Dáil debate of the following week but, when it all happened in the Four Courts, it was presented as an open and shut case to the family and living victims of the atrocity.

That something was happening, and that it was serious, was obvious to seasoned court watchers, as well as legal and police force personnel, when an adjournment was called as the case moved into February. What had gone before was the refusal of one prosecution witness to give evidence, the plea from two more witnesses that they could not remember what had gone on in their home the night before the killing, and then the 'trial within a trial'. That involved the statements that Garda witnesses testified had been made in custody by John Quinn, who the state prosecution acknowledged was a bit-part player in the crime. What was being thrashed out in evidence and intense cross-examination, was whether the statements made by Quinn would be allowed to be entered as evidence for consideration by the three judges.

The broad hint that the trial could be taking a new twist came from Quinn's barrister, Ms Eilis McDermott. When applying for the Tuesday adjournment, she told the judges, 'There has been a certain development.'

That night an urgent message went through to Limerick to Ann McCabe and her brother-in-law, Pat Kearney, who was looking after the public aspects of the McCabe family during, what was for them, an increasingly distressing time. They were being summoned to Dublin for the next day's hearing. The import of the message was that the prospect of securing a murder conviction was now out of sight, and that the Adare gang could very well walk from the Special Criminal Court.

As they recall the events of the next morning, the slow legal process that they had followed in the trial suddenly changed to overdrive urgency. Everything was now happening so fast that they could hardly follow and absorb what was being said to them. The situation was not helped by the fact that Ben O'Sullivan was not there in time for the briefing by the legal team and Garda leaders of the Adare investigation. On the outskirts of Dublin, the car he was travelling in was involved in a minor collision which delayed him and meant that he was returning to the court where he had faced his partner's killers with no real advance explanation of the shock that awaited him.

As the family remembers it, through a haze of what was close to disbelief and verging on unreality, they were, in the words of Pat Kearney, 'bustled' into a ground floor consultation room. There, the State prosecution rapidly summarised the position that the trial had arrived at. The position as set out to the family, and which was to be put before the court in the subsequent hours, was that a conviction for capital murder was not certain. Having reached that point of uncertainty in the case, and the possibility that the men in the dock could go free, a plea of manslaughter was being accepted from those accused of taking part in the killing.

Numb with shock, Ann McCabe was in a virtual trance state. What was being said by the legal team and the senior Gardaí was too much to take in. She could not understand what was happening. But Pat Kearney was asking questions about the plea of guilty to manslaughter. He and Ann McCabe and the other members of the family had their shock somewhat relieved with assurances that the manslaughter conviction would bring down sentences of 20-25 years in jail.

Due to the hurried briefing and consultations that had been taking place, the resumption of the case was held up by ten minutes. When the judges took their seats before the full assembly of legal teams, the men in the dock, the McCabe family and a large number of detectives who had been involved in the case, yet another delay and adjournment took place. The Senior Counsel leading the state prosecution, Edward Comyn, applied for a 30 minute adjournment to allow new charges to be brought.

It was 11.50 a.m. on Wednesday, 3 February, when the court resumed again. Detective Inspector John Kerin, who had led the Garda investigation extending over more than two years, gave evidence of re-arraigning the four accused of capital murder with the new charge of manslaughter. Mr Comyn then asked each of the four to be re-arraigned. One by one they stood up and when the charge of capital murder was put to them, each replied, 'Not guilty to murder, guilty to manslaughter.' They also pleaded guilty to new charges of maliciously wounding Detective Garda Ben O'Sullivan, and having firearms with intent to commit a robbery in Adare on 7 June 1996.

In the Dáil chamber six days later, during the special debate on the trial and its outcome, the Fine Gael spokesman on justice, Deputy Jim Higgins, gave his verdict. 'From a situation of total denial of their involvement in the killing of Garda McCabe, the four accused changed their plea. Essentially they said they were at the scene, had guns and killed Garda McCabe, but did not mean it.'

When telling the court that the pleas were acceptable to the Director of Public Prosecutions, Mr Comyn entered a *nolle prosequi* on behalf of the State on outstanding charges. This meant that the charges against the four of membership of the IRA, possession of arms and ammunition, and of conspiracy, were not being proceeded with.

Pearse McCauley, Michael O'Neill and Jeremiah Sheehy wore suits, shirts and ties, and had green prisoner ribbons on their lapels. Kevin Walsh wore a green fleece jacket, shirt and tie.

The fifth man, John Quinn, pleaded guilty to conspiracy to commit a robbery in Adare between 5-8 June 1996.

The following day, Mr Comyn told the court the reasons why the State consented to accept the guilty to manslaughter pleas.

The key element of what the prosecuting counsel had to say was that there was not enough evidence, either from what had already been heard in the trial, or from the remaining evidence, to establish the criminal intent necessary for murder convictions.

While verbal admissions could have been construed as admitting involvement in the crime, there were no admissions of discharging the gun, and none of being involved in the plan or intent to kill Detective Garda McCabe. It was not possible to ascribe any particular role to any of the defendants in the discharge of the gun. There was no evidence of who fired the fatal shots from the Kalashnikov assault rifle that killed Detective Garda McCabe. He did say that Gardaí did not believe that Pearse McCauley had fired the shots.

While the court had already been appraised of the facts of the case, the remaining evidence would have connected the accused men with the events surrounding the Adare shooting.

In summary, Mr Comyn said, 'Looking at the evidence, the three counts that the four men have pleaded guilty to are appropriate.'

He said that manslaughter ranged from negligence to something short of murder, and the offence before the court was at the upper end of the scale.

Outside the precinct of the court, Detective Inspector John Kerin said that the refusal of the Tipperary farmer, Patrick Harty, to give evidence of sheltering the Adare gang on his property, had ended any real chances the prosecution had of securing capital murder convictions. While Harty had informed Gardaí of a change of heart and willingness to give evidence for the prosecution, the State legal counsel took the view that such evidence would be virtually useless. The defence would have argued that the evidence of John Harty would have been provided under duress of the prison sentence he had received for contempt of the court.

Inspector Kerin said the substitution of the manslaughter charges in place of capital murder had been forced on the prosecution because of IRA intimidation. 'We still had a reasonable amount of evidence against them but, at that stage when Patrick Harty refused to give evidence, we knew we were in difficulty.'

The Garda Commissioner, Pat Byrne, also pointed to intimidation of witnesses but expressed himself satisfied that an admission had been secured from those responsible for the killing of Detective Jerry McCabe.

'We set out to bring those responsible before the courts. I was pleased to hear these people who killed Jerry McCabe admit in the courts that they were the people who did it. That justified all of our actions in pursuing them throughout the country,' the Commissioner said.

While the legal and Garda members of the prosecution team had outlined the motivation for accepting the guilty of manslaughter plea in wrapping up the Special Criminal Court hearing, greater detail and depth was added by the Minister for Justice in the special Dáil debate which followed the weekend outcry about the trial outcome.

Before going into how the plea bargain came about and who was and was not involved in the process, Minister John O'Donoghue provided guidance for the Dáil on precise aspects of the matters under debate.

He made the point that in the Irish judicial system, unlike other jurisdictions, the judge or judges in a case have no part in any arrangement to do with pleas that may be settled on by the opposing sides. He also provided the Dáil with the expert views of the Law Reform Commission in its consultation paper on sentencing. While conceding that negotiated agreement on court pleas in Ireland tended to be in relatively minor cases, the Law Reform Commission had listed the practical benefits of plea bargaining in its recommendations and advice to government. In that context, the Minster said, the report on sentencing had mentioned that where plea bargaining took place, 'the result is certain and may be preferable to the possibility of the accused person being acquitted of a number of charges or of a more serious charge.'

In what he described as 'one of the most difficult and sensitive decisions which the Director of Public Prosecutions has ever been called upon to make', the Minister explained why the prosecution had decided in favour of 'the certainty of a conviction'.

While conceding that it was 'a matter of regret and disappointment', the Minister added, 'the highly experienced prosecution team found themselves in a situation where, on the basis of their own professional analysis, an insistence on holding to the murder charge carried an unacceptably high risk of failure.'

The Minister also asked the Dáil, in the interests of balance, to contemplate the alternative scenario of what would have transpired if a different course had been taken. He asked the deputies to think about what the reaction would have been if the trial had resulted in acquittal, with the accused walking free, and then it emerging that the Director of Public Prosecutions could have gone down the plea bargain road and secured a conviction on the manslaughter charge. 'We have to ask ourselves honestly if the public concern or criticism would have been any the lesser had events taken that course instead,' he said.

The sequence of events in the consultation rooms behind the scenes at the Special Criminal Court were set out for the Dáil by the Minister.

On the basis of consultations with the legal team conducting the State prosecution, and the facts and circumstances that had started to unfold as the trial went on, the Director of Public Prosecutions had to make a judgement.

Discussions had taken place between the legal teams for the prosecution and the defence, during which the defence indicated that the accused would plead guilty to manslaughter on the understanding that the murder charge would not be proceeded with. The Minister added, 'It was obviously the prosecutors' professional judgement that the right course was to opt for the certainty of conviction, rather than run what was judged to be the unacceptable risk if the murder charge was insisted upon, that the killers would walk free.'

The Minister pointed out to the Dáil that it was not the case that the Director of Public Prosecutions would set charges to be brought in court at a higher level so that a lesser charge would gain a guilty plea. 'The DPP brings forward a charge on the basis that he can prove it,' the Minister declared. 'The DPP would only agree to a lesser charge where he was not satisfied that the higher charge could be established.'

The Minister said also that the senior Gardaí involved in the case 'were kept fully abreast of what was judged by the lawyers to be the appropriate course before the decision to accept the plea was made'.

In subsequent exchanges during the special Dáil debate, the Minister faced opposition questioning on the originating points that brought about the State consent to the manslaughter charge.

The Minister stated that the prosecution team was led by one of the most experienced criminal lawyers in the country with vast experience of such cases. 'He advised on how the matter should progress in conjunction with other members of the legal team.'

'The decision to accept a plea of manslaughter was honestly reached,' the Minister stated. 'It was not influenced by any extraneous viewpoint. There was no involvement whatsoever by me as Minister, the Taoiseach, or anybody else politically, in the decision reached by the Director of Public Prosecutions.'

Having told the Dáil that he had no direct involvement, influence or bearing on the case, the Minister said that he had not been directly informed about the decision to accept the lesser plea.

Minister O'Donoghue told the Dáil that it was his information that the acceptance of the manslaughter plea had been conveyed to the Attorney General's office on the night before the court announcement, and had been conveyed by the Director of Public Prosecution's office 'as a matter of courtesy'.

The Minister said it was his understanding that the Attorney General had not been informed until the following morning, and the Attorney General, in turn, had tried to communicate the matter to the Taoiseach. But the Taoiseach was attending a meeting and did not learn about the turn of events in the Special Criminal Court until after the guilty of manslaughter plea had been accepted.

The Taoiseach, Bertie Ahern, had been meeting with the Northern Secretary, Mo Mowlam, that day and commented on the outcome of the trial in the context of the manslaughter plea and the public campaign of political pressure to have the killers included under the prisoner release provisions of the Good Friday Agreement.

The Taoiseach termed the plea bargained guilty to manslaughter pleas 'controversial' and said he understood the anger of the public. 'They [the public] wanted the case to go through,' the Taoiseach said and pledged that the four who pleaded guilty would not be released under the Good Friday Agreement. The Taoiseach also made it clear that he and members of his Cabinet had absolutely no involvement in the State prosecution consent to the manslaughter charge and plea. He said that the decision taken by the Director of Public Prosecutions, Eamonn Barnes, had been taken without any consultation with the government.

The head of the body representing rank and file Gardaí was reflecting the reaction of the organisation when he said he was incensed at the prosecution's decision. President of the Garda Representative Body, John Healy, said, 'as far as this organisation is concerned, Detective Jerry McCabe was murdered.'

Fury and dismay at the outcome was publicly registered by two Dáil Deputies for the Limerick East constituency who, as former Ministers for Justice, had received security protection from the dead detective and his partner. Both Des O'Malley and Michael Noonan called for 30-year jail terms on the eve of the sentencing by the Special Criminal Court. A long-time adversary of subversives, O'Malley pointed out, 'Every one of these people are members of the Sinn Féin party, and that party failed to condemn the murder.'

Voices were raised to new levels of frustration the following day when the sentences were handed down. But the presiding judge was unhappy too, and said the public comments that followed the guilty pleas 'did nothing to serve either the interests of the law as it stands, or justice'.

Sentenced to terms in prison of between 11 and 14 years, dictated by additional charges against two, were the four who had pleaded guilty to manslaughter. The presiding judge, Mr Justice Johnson, pointed out that the offence of manslaughter varied from death resulting from serious negligence upwards and told the court:

> *This case, quite clearly, is one of the most serious forms of manslaughter. The robbery, in the course of which the offences were committed to which the pleas of guilty have been entered, was well planned and carried out with military precision.*

Before handing down sentences, the judges heard pleas for mitigation from the legal team for the defence. Mr Justice Johnson said that Sheehy, O'Neill and McCauley had expressed regret for the death of Detective Garda McCabe. 'But the court notes the fact that no regret regarding the death of Detective McCabe or the wounding of Detective O'Sullivan was expressed by Walsh or on his behalf,' the judge said.

Kevin Walsh and Pearse McCauley, both of whom had firearms in their possession and resisted arrest when captured, received sentences of 14 years. Jailed for terms of 11 years were Jeremiah Sheehy and Michael O'Neill.

The fifth defendant, John Quinn, who had pleaded guilty to conspiracy to commit a robbery, was jailed for six years.

The McCabe family made no comment whatever on the outcome of the case but reserved what the media generally described as 'a dignified silence' in the traumatic aftermath of the trial.

A prepared statement on behalf of the family was read outside the Four Courts by Pat Kearney, brother-in-law, fellow Kerryman, and onetime Garda colleague of Jerry McCabe.

The statement said:

> *The father, family, wife and children of the late Detective Garda Jerry McCabe offer their most sincere thanks and appreciation to all those who supported them through the ordeal of the past 31 months since Jerry was gunned down in Adare.*
>
> *The family has been consoled by the steadfast support of the Garda Síochána at all levels, especially the support of Jerry's former colleagues, by the outpouring of care from relatives, friends and neighbours and by the spontaneous messages and gestures of sympathy received from all parts and all sections of the country. The family has been deeply touched by the outpouring of feelings of solidarity which have flowed unceasingly since Jerry's death.*
>
> *Deep feelings of gratitude and friendship are extended to Detective Garda Ben O'Sullivan, his wife Ann and their family. He will always have a place among the McCabe family who wish him every blessing and gladness in a full and long life.*
>
> *Most heartfelt thanks go to the Gardaí for their single-minded pursuit of those who admitted their responsibility for taking the life of Jerry McCabe. It is a matter of pride that Jerry's Garda colleagues in Limerick never rested until his killers were brought to justice.*
>
> *The family also extends gratitude to all those involved in the successful prosecution of the case. Because of the brutal circumstances involved, the family of the late Detective Garda McCabe has had to deal with their grief in public view. The family now wishes to cope with the loss by private grieving as a family.*

After more than two and a half years, and a trial that stretched over three weeks, the torment for Ann McCabe and her extended family was only beginning.

Chapter 13

It is difficult to pinpoint any single killing over almost 30 years of the northern conflict that would have a more devastating and prolonged impact for all concerned than the Adare shooting of Detective Jerry McCabe.

The death had an unprecedented, destabilising impact that served to keep the horror of Adare and the name of Jerry McCabe to the forefront of events in a highly charged political process and what seemed endless rounds of talks, negotiations and trading that widened to international dimensions. For the widow and extended family of the detective whose life had been blown away, their trauma and anguish was to be prolonged by circumstances and events entirely outside their control, but in which they found themselves embroiled.

Jerry McCabe died on duty as a Garda. But, as the IRA and its media machine always protested, members of the defence forces of the Republic were specifically excluded as targets of military action by the volunteers of the IRA. The killing took place in the Republic where the IRA was not supposed to be engaged in conflict with the defence forces or any other forces. So, in a conventional war, would it have stood as a killing in a neutral country, where the casualty would not have any reason either to expect to come under attack, or the need to prepare to take defensive action?

The shock of the first killing in 11 years of a member of the defence forces of the Republic was nationwide and genuine. However, for some elements the shock that would have the most telling consequences was the shock to the system.

The twisting steel of the Kalashnikov rounds that tore the life breath out of the detective also riddled the fabric of a political process that had been painstakingly assembled over a period of years, and was at an exceptionally fragile stage.

The secret talks that had initiated with nationalists but picked up other interests along the way, had primarily achieved a halt in the armed struggle of the IRA, thereby forcing the hands of others to at least keep the peace.

Even the terminology for the break in the IRA's use of force campaign was a matter of extreme sensitivity. Lest it should be perceived or misrepresented as a permanent halt or, worse still, interpreted as a sign of weakness or weakening of purpose in republican ranks, a formula or code had to be brought into play.

For the general public unacquainted with the subtleties involved, it was a ceasefire. But in other quarters it was referred to as the 'cessation', and within the republican movement as the 'sos', employing the Irish word for a break or rest which can be interpreted as a spell of inaction for taking a breather, recharging the batteries or, in the parlance of antiquity, for preparation for action, the girding of loins. The key inference was that it was temporary or an interim tactic.

The 'sos' was not so much contrived as engineered in the search for an exit from the Northern Ireland scene of strife. It would also serve in opening the way towards an end of conflict without loss of face on all sides.

The opportunity had been prepared in endless hours stretched over long years of exchanges and position papers geared to establish common ground without having to give ground.

The 'sos' began as a summer break in hostilities. It was presented as something akin to a trial run that would not go on for more than a few months. But a test run also involves samples, and the taste of life without violent conflict proved sweeter and more palatable than the diet of bitterness that had gone before.

Once in place and experienced as a new dimension to living, the real poser for those who distrusted it was how to put an end to it. There were not just sceptics, but very convinced opponents on all sides against the 'sos' and its agenda. Within the security authorities there were deep-rooted suspicions that what was being presented as a move away from conflict was, in fact, a smokescreen behind which the paramilitaries were preparing, training and arming for the next phase of the armed struggle. On the nationalist side, and particularly among use of force adherents in the republican movement, there were clearly expressed apprehensions. The fear was that the break in hostilities would be used by the security authorities and their clandestine networks to smoke out volunteers and other activists, and to gather security intelligence to be put to use at the first opportunity.

The 'sos' became operative in August 1994 and held for 17 months. But while bullets and bombs were unheard in the new peaceful air of Northern Ireland, behind the scenes the republican movement was in turmoil.

As the 'sos' lengthened, so did the distance between the uppermost figures in the political and paramilitary wings of republicanism. As the tensions within the republican movement stretched, at times to near breaking point, the Irish and UK Governments, and the US administration of President Bill Clinton, brought their influences to bear. Keeping the peace was of the utmost priority. In the laborious but covert laying down of the peace process groundwork, channels of communication had been opened up so that when things got hot inside the republican movement or other quarters, measures to cool the situation, or divert attention and energies elsewhere, could be brought into play. The over-riding objective was to tend, feed and facilitate the growth of the newborn peace and to clear and ease the way so that it could develop and mature.

Peace in the North and the difference it was making was being played up. But each passing month of peace was stretching the patience of the militarists of the republican movement. The threat that the peace would be broken was overshadowed by the spectre of a split or splintering of the republicans which would beget a new force driven by the armed policy, and leave the advocates of electoral politics stranded in no man's land.

The incubator treatment meant that keeping the peace and the means for maintaining it became the imperative. In keeping the 'sos' going against fierce internal resistance and opposition, the republican leadership had brought communication with the other interests involved to new levels. It was essential for outside interests to have a clear understanding of what could and could not be attempted at any one time; to realise how far certain elements could be pushed; and to accept that internal negotiations and debates also required a willingness to compromise.

The 'sos' held for most of 18 months because understanding and trust held up.

Even before the bombs and bullets were heard again, the stress on the 'sos' was being flagged to partners in the peace alliance. Intelligence networks were picking up clear signs that the physical force camp in the republican movement was in the ascendancy and that a return to the armed struggle was on the way.

First came Canary Wharf. The huge truck bomb explosion in London's docklands killed two and devastated a prime commercial property area of the English capital with damage estimated at £100 million. It was detonated at 7.00 p.m. on 9 February. It served to shake up British public opinion and remind John Major's government that the IRA had not gone away.

Nine days later, 21 year old Edward O'Brien from Gorey in county Wexford died and five others were injured when a bomb in a carrier bag exploded prematurely as he boarded a London bus in Aldwych in the city centre. When he died O'Brien was carrying a Walther handgun. A search of his London home uncovered 15 kilos of Semtex plastic explosive, 20 timers, four detonators, an incendiary device and ammunition for the handgun. A Semtex bomb, similar to the device that killed O'Brien, had been found some days before in a telephone box at Charing Cross Road, also in the centre of the city.

The IRA claimed O'Brien as a volunteer and the newspaper *An Phoblacht/Republican News* reported that O'Brien had been in place and under cover for two years without coming to the attention of the security authorities.

Although his family in Wexford issued a statement condemning 'unreservedly' all paramilitary organisations and requested no paramilitary trappings at the funeral, that death was to dent confidence in the efforts for peace that had been taking place since the autumn of 1994. The bomb, the bomb making equipment and the undetected presence of O'Brien in the UK for two years meant that the IRA had a 'sleeper' in place throughout the period of the 'sos'.

In the knowledge that a return to armed warfare by the IRA would automatically herald a resumption of operations by the subversives specialising in fundraising activities, detectives and Gardaí of the Limerick division thwarted an early return to armed hold-ups when seizing a fleet of vehicles during the Christmas/New Year season of 1995-96.

The armed struggle came back onto the streets of the Republic with shocking lethal force on a June morning in Adare with the gunning down of Detective Jerry McCabe. That killing also dealt a potentially mortal blow to the peace building that had taken place during the 'sos'.

Such was the preoccupation of all parties involved in assembling and preserving a peace framework that allowances were made for aberrations and for breakdowns when matters either went out of control, or when the reins were loosened in the interests of not losing entire control.

British trust in what they regarded as a ceasefire was deeply unsettled by the shooting dead of postal worker Frank Kerr (53) in Newry as the 'sos' entered its third month on 10 November 1994.

When three armed men dressed as postal workers entered the Newry sorting office and tied up a number of staff, Frank Kerr resisted. He struggled with one of the raiders and was shot in the head, dying two days later in hospital. 20 years previously the same Frank Kerr had been through the terror of an armed IRA fundraising attack. In 1973, the Catholic bachelor from Camlough in south Armagh had been abducted and held for four days during an armed robbery of his Royal Mail delivery van.

In a sequence of events that would be replicated by the Adare crime, the IRA Army Council initially disowned the Newry killing and robbery of £131,000. The President of Sinn Féin, Gerry Adams, went on public record to say he was shocked by the killing.

With the security authorities satisfied that the operation had been carried out by the south Armagh IRA, the 'sos' or ceasefire was at serious risk. The British government was strengthening its resolve that IRA decommissioning was a must. South of the border, the government of the Republic was putting on hold its plans for introduction of early release of republican prisoners. In the meantime, hectic moves and manoeuvres were going on behind the scenes to carry out running repairs on the peace process.

It would be ten days before the IRA acknowledged that the raid and killing was the work of their members. There also followed an apology from the group responsible to the family of Frank Kerr, stating that the unarmed postal worker had been shot 'in an intense scuffle'.

In what would also foreshadow Adare and its fallout, the IRA claimed that there had been a breakdown in its chain of command. 'Those carrying out the robbery were acting on instructions, but the so-called operation had not been sanctioned by the IRA leadership,' the statement said. 'Responsibility for this incident lies with an identified problem in the army's chain of command, not with the volunteers involved. This has now been rectified,' the statement added.

The Newry armed hold-up and killing of Frank Kerr was explained away to the media by republican sources as an aberration. But the action served a multitude of purposes besides its ostensible fundraising objective. Although the raid and fatal shooting severely undermined the trust and confidence that had been gaining ground on the British and Irish Government sides, it also sent out a number of other messages. It sent out a clear statement that whatever deal or arrangement had been arrived at, or brokered by the political leadership of the republican movement, it would be presumptuous to assume that the same leadership had absolute control over those directly involved in the armed struggle which was supposed to be suspended. On the other hand, the Newry robbery and loss of a civilian's life could also be cited by the republican leadership as an example of the volatile situation and people they were attempting to keep in line when pressing for allowances to be made by the British and Irish governments, and the US administration.

The killing of Frank Kerr occurred when the 'sos' was just three months old. The killing of Detective Jerry McCabe happened four months after the resumption of the armed struggle. In each case, the response of the IRA Army Council was to initially disown those responsible for the killings and to deny that the operations had been sanctioned. But in both cases, the killers would be acknowledged within the following fortnight as members of the IRA with fudged explanations fed to the media as to how the shootings from one side only occurred. It was noteworthy that in the Newry killing, an apology was tendered by those involved to the family of the dead Frank Kerr. No similar expression was offered to the widow and family of a member of the Garda force in the Republic.

The killing of Detective Jerry McCabe and the fate of his killers, as they were first hunted down and then brought to justice, became inextricably linked with the political events that took place after 7 June 1996 in the quest for an end to the northern conflict.

There was a change of government in the Republic in June 1997 with the new Taoiseach, Bertie Ahern, setting out terms for another ceasefire in the North that would cause turmoil in the IRA and republican movement. By the end of that year the strains and tensions between the different camps in the IRA finally brought about a new split and the formation of the Real IRA. But, by year end, Sinn Féin had entered into all-party talks at Stormont and subscribed to the six principles for non-violence set out by former US Senate Leader, George Mitchell, to clear the way for the Good Friday Agreement signed in Belfast on 10 May 1998.

Early releases of republican and other paramilitary prisoners had started in 1998, before the IRA men arrested and charged with the Adare killing were brought to trial in the opening months of 1999, prompting Sinn Féin statements that they would qualify for early release.

The road to full decommissioning that the IRA finally agreed to in April 2005 would prove exceptionally rocky, and every bump reverberated in Limerick to pain and bruise the widow and family of the last Garda to be shot down by republican paramilitaries. Every pitfall, snag and glitch in the on-off talks and negotiations continually brought the Adare killing into the frame. Played out over the 1998-2005 period, with cards held close to chests around the negotiation tables, each time the stakes were raised from the republican side, the card thrown down was certain to include the release of the Adare killers.

Chapter 14

The disbelief and fury that greeted the plea bargain under which the Adare killers were convicted of the lesser charge of manslaughter was compounded by the sentences handed down the following day.

In Limerick city, where the slain detective had served and made a home for his family, Gardaí and the local deputy and Minister of State voiced the deepest concern and unhappiness.

'This is absolutely and completely unbelievable,' was the comment from Garda Paul Browne, regional member of the Garda Representative Association who told the media that other members of the force had conveyed to him their deep anger and dismay. Garda Browne qualified his remarks by saying that the GRA accepted that the law had to take its course and 'if a court of law makes a decision, that is accepted'.

Minister of State at the Department of Education, Willie O'Dea, professed himself 'absolutely furious' with the turn of events and unhappy that plea bargaining had been employed in relation to such a horrific crime. He reflected concerns that had emerged during the trial when calling for measures to protect witnesses throughout trials and for a reasonable period afterwards.

But Minister O'Dea and the GRA were to be disappointed with the following day's sentences on the four IRA men. Minister O'Dea had called in advance for sentences to match 'the horrible nature of the crime'. In the wake of the court ruling, the GRA acting General Secretary, PJ Stone, said that life sentences should have been imposed, with a minimum of 20 years imprisonment. He said:

> The Association is of the view that the sentences do not in any way reflect the severity of the crimes. People who by their own admission have accepted their culpability and guilt in the unlawful killing of a Garda colleague had not been treated severely enough.

With the Sinn Féin chief negotiator, Martin McGuinness, drawing widespread condemnation for initiating a relentless campaign for early release of the killers before the judges of the Special Criminal Court handed down the sentences, the GRA was pressing for government reassurances of the highest order.

The GRA leader called on the Taoiseach to place on the record of the Dáil that the early release terms of the Good Friday Agreement would not apply to those sentenced for the Adare killing. He warned of a crisis in the ranks of the Gardaí when calling on the Taoiseach to advise the Sinn Féin leaders that their statements on early release were 'both inaccurate and misleading'.

'Furious' too was Limerick's most prominent member of the Dáil, Des O'Malley, who, as Minister for Justice, had confronted the subversion threat to the state following the outbreak of hostilities in Northern Ireland. He shared the fury about Sinn Féin taking to the broadcasting airways immediately before and after the Adare sentences were delivered and stepping up claims for inclusion under the British-Irish agreement for early release by April 2000.

The solicitor turned politician also had words for the presiding trial judge who had criticised public comment about the decision of the Director of Public Prosecutions to accept the manslaughter plea.

'Quite honestly, it was quite unreal of the judge to expect that people would not comment. The case was effectively over and there was no jury involved,' Deputy O'Malley asserted.

A very different approach was indicated by the former leader of the Progressive Democrats party which was then on the opposition benches. Recalling that one of those sentenced for the Adare killing had been given early release by Minister Nora Owen during the Rainbow Government administration, O'Malley noted that, 'both governments seem to be anxious to placate these people.'

Exceptionally strong sentiments expressed in the wake of the trial by the Association of Garda Chief Superintendents were read into the record of the Dáil by the Fine Gael justice spokesman, Jim Higgins, who pointed out that the statement came from 'the most senior Garda officers in the state – a responsible and cautious organisation not given to flights of fancy'.

The statement from the top Garda officers read:

> *The Association believes that the murder of Detective Garda McCabe was a deliberate act committed by ruthless, practiced and dedicated terrorists. The sentence imposed on those individuals does not reflect the seriousness of the crime committed, nor does it serve as a warning to those who might follow their example. What occurred in Adare was an attack on one of the institutions of the State, the Garda Síochána, by a private army raised and maintained by the republican movement. What occurred in the Special Criminal Court was the same people taking on the criminal justice system of the State. They won on both occasions.*

In the Dáil debate of the following week, the Fine Gael leader, John Bruton, led the chorus of dismay and disapproval from the two main opposition parties.

Deputy Bruton, who was the serving Taoiseach at the time of the Adare killing and attended the requiem Mass for the slain detective, did not mince words:

> *Detective Garda Jerry McCabe was murdered. Legalistic semantics do not alter the fact. He was murdered by a heavily armed gang in most brutal and callous circumstances when 15 shots were fired into his car. It is an insult to a brave and dedicated officer and his colleagues, who continue to stand in the front line in preserving our State, to say that it was anything but murder.*
>
> *It was a calculated assault on one of the most esteemed symbols of our democracy, the badge of the Garda Síochána, by the military wing of a political party which is represented in this house and which aspires to sharing power in the government of Northern Ireland.*

The scathing tone of Deputy Bruton's contribution was matched, if not surpassed, by his party's spokesman on justice, Deputy Jim Higgins:

> *The decision by the State to accept a reduced plea of manslaughter in what was manifestly a murder, a capital murder at that, was*

wrong. It represents an unacceptable compromise and strikes at the heart of the criminal justice system. This was a case where there was a clear challenge to the authority and institutions of the State and the State lost. Seldom, if ever, has an outcome to a court case been greeted with such disquiet and universal public revulsion.

Deputy Higgins was equally blunt when delivering his verdict on the abrupt ending of the trial and acceptance of the manslaughter plea. 'It was a wrong decision,' he said.

He went on to say:

If ever there was a case of cold blooded murder, this was it. It was a planned, fully fledged Provisional IRA raid. Balaclavas and Kalashnikovs were used and a barrage of gunfire was fired into the body of a Garda, not in self defence, but with the intention of killing him and anybody else who got in their way. The intent was clear and how any State prosecution doubted its ability to prove it is beyond me.

Deputy Higgins had compelling questions to pose to the government and the Dáil.

Besides the whys and wherefores of how the State had consented to accept the guilty of manslaughter plea, he queried why the decision had not been left to the three judges of the Special Criminal Court. 'There was little forensic but strong circumstantial evidence. Why were the judges not allowed to draw their own conclusions and inferences from the book of evidence as presented from the strong circumstantial evidence and clear evidence of blatant intimidation?' he asked.

He also drew attention to another option that had been available to the prosecution. Instead of accepting a plea to a reduced charge of manslaughter, he explained that 1990 legislation provided that if evidence did not support a conviction for capital murder, the murder alternative could be brought in. 'The State should have vigorously pressed the capital murder charge and it would not have risked all being lost,' he contended.

Blame was being squarely placed on the State and the government by the Labour spokesman on justice, Deputy Brendan Howlin, who had harsh words for the Director of Public Prosecutions.

Stating that the government had seriously misread the mood of the public in relation to what he called 'the extraordinary situation' which led the DPP to accept pleas of guilty, he added that, besides the sympathy for the McCabe family, 'there is also a sense of anger and frustration among the public at what it sees as a serious failure in our legal system.'

'The law may well have taken its course, but justice has not been done,' he declared and gave his reason. 'The public finds it impossible to reconcile the acceptance by the State of a guilty plea to charges of manslaughter with the graphic account of the violent death of Detective McCabe given to the Special Criminal Court.'

He made the point that 'to all of us the term manslaughter means causing the unintentional death of somebody, perhaps through carelessness or omission'. He then asked the Dáil, 'How does this compare with the events of Adare on 7 June 1996?'

Recalling the evidence of the shooting that had been presented to the Special Criminal Court, Deputy Howlin said, 'By any standards what happened in Adare was premeditated brutal murder and the inability of the State to secure a single conviction for murder is a serious failure of our legal system.'

The Labour deputy also had severe words to say to Sinn Féin. He advised the party that it was in danger of having its good work in negotiation of the British-Irish Agreement 'washed away by a tide of revulsion'.

That revulsion was caused, he contended, 'not just by the attitude of the republican movement to the murder of Detective McCabe and the subsequent trial, but also to the continued daily accounts of punishment mutilations in Northern Ireland and refusal to make any movement on decommissioning'.

The observations contributed by both Deputy Jim Higgins and Deputy Howlin to the Dáil debate were anticipated, in part, by a solicitor then with the Dublin criminal law practice of Dermot H Morris & Co.

In a commentary-analysis article published in *The Examiner* in the immediate aftermath of the plea change, Pa Daly acknowledged that he did not wish to speculate on why the manslaughter pleas proved acceptable. But he stated:

> *On the face of it, it is strange to see how a murder charge was not proceeded with in circumstances where four men with loaded weapons go to carry out a robbery in which Detective Garda McCabe was killed. Manslaughter may have been acceptable if some members of the gang did not know that the others were carrying arms, or if they had agreed beforehand not to harm anyone. It could be argued that the probable result of carrying automatic weapons to a robbery is death or serious injury.*

The view that the courts had proved wanting in the eyes of the public would endure and be re-echoed almost three years later by a churchman with first hand experience of the horror and anguish of the Adare shooting.

The Rev Stephen Neill was curate of the Limerick parish and also the Church of Ireland Chaplain to Limerick Regional Hospital. He received a call from the sexton at twelfth century St Mary's Cathedral telling him of the shooting in Adare and that one of the Gardaí had already been taken to the hospital in the Raheen suburb of the city.

At the hospital, where he conveyed his condolences and tried to comfort the seriously wounded Detective Ben O'Sullivan, he witnessed scenes which, he said, 'will always remain with me'.

The Rev Neill shared his experience and thoughts in a letter to *The Irish Times* in 1999 when he felt compelled to respond to an earlier letter defending what was described as 'a robbery gone wrong', and which also suggested that the dissatisfaction of political leaders and their parties with the manslaughter verdict was undermining the integrity of the judicial process. He wrote:

> *Extraordinary situations call for extraordinary measures and certainly nothing was more extraordinary than the farce which marked the latter stages of the McCabe murder trial.*
>
> *In the light of what happened we have to ask what we can do to redeem the situation for the members of the Garda who continue to defend our peace while increasingly uncertain of the protection that*

the courts will be able to afford them. The very least we owe them is justice when they have given their lives in the line of duty. The sentiments expressed by our Taoiseach and others after the verdicts were an attempt to right the wrong, to do justice to the memory of Jerry McCabe – a justice which our judicial system failed miserably to provide.

Chapter 15

The Garda file on the Adare shooting is not closed. That the file remained open was announced on the fifth day of the 1999 trial when it was disclosed by the prosecution that two people were then being hunted. Since then, it has emerged that one of those wanted for questioning was actually contracted to a state-funded overseas aid agency and was believed by Gardaí to have returned to his homeland to take part in the IRA operation in Adare.

In addition to the two mentioned, but not by name, to the Special Criminal Court whose fingerprints had been found on the Mitsubishi Lancer getaway car, investigating Gardaí were satisfied that other subversives had roles, however small, to play in the lead-up and tidying away of weapons and equipment in the days after the shooting. Known republican activists and sympathisers were searched out as the net of the investigation spread virtually countrywide from Limerick. In the process, important information was gathered during thousands of interrogations and taking of statements. In some instances information was freely given because of a sense of revulsion. In other cases scruples, brought on through guilt by association among some who had identified with the republican movement and its paramilitary wing, helped to loosen tongues.

The fact that at least two men had taken refuge overseas had been known before it was confirmed to the Adare trial by George Bermingham BL, one of the State prosecution legal team. Less than four weeks later, one of those who had fled to South America was named under the privilege of the Dáil.

During the special Dáil debate on the outcome of the Adare trial which took place on 9 February 1999, the Fine Gael spokesperson on justice, Deputy Jim Higgins, named the wanted man as Paul Damery, and said Damery was working with the Agency for Personal Service Overseas (APSO) in Nicaragua.

APSO was a State-sponsored agency and was then part of Ireland Aid, the government's overseas development assistance programme which came under the Department of Foreign Affairs. In supporting the work of Irish and international non-government organisations working in developing countries, APSO recruited qualified and experienced personnel for assignments in developing countries. With the aim of transferring skills and supporting local communities and their organisations to reduce poverty and promote economic and social development, those contracted by APSO tended to be drawn from sectors ranging from education, administration, business and engineering, to trades, health, social sciences, agriculture and environment.

Paul Damery was an electrician from Cobh in county Cork from a family with a strong republican pedigree. His brother, Ciarán, had been one of the members of the Irish National Liberation Army (INLA) captured with their leader, Dominic McGlinchy, after a fierce gun battle outside Newmarket-on-Fergus in Clare in the early hours of St Patrick's Day, 1984.

It took over two years for information to come into the public arena that Damery was on the wanted list of those who Gardaí wished to question about the Adare killing. But, as it became clear that the matter was likely to be raised in the Dáil, the chief executive of APSO, Paul Beggan, issued a statement on 20 November 1998. That was less than two months before the Adare trial got underway.

The statement pointed out that while Paul Damery was on assignment for APSO in Central America, he was not employed directly by the agency. At that time he was working with INATEC, a government organisation in Nicaragua. APSO, its chief executive explained, supported the assignment by providing living allowances.

The statement added:

> *In October 1996, the Gardaí informed APSO that they wished to interview Mr Damery regarding a serious criminal offence. At that time Mr Damery was in Nicaragua. The Gardaí asked APSO to provide information on the whereabouts and work of Mr Damery; this was provided to them. On a number of occasions since then, APSO have been asked to update that information and have done so. In addition APSO has voluntarily informed the Gardaí of any*

*change in Mr Damery's situation. APSO has at all times co-
operated with the Gardaí. APSO understands, however, that no
contact has been made by the authorities with Mr Damery.*

The APSO chief executive's statement of November 1998 also
stated that Damery had started work in Central America in 1991 and
that his fixed term contract was due to end in June 1999.

When he raised the Damery and APSO issue in the Dáil during
the February special debate, Deputy Jim Higgins commented, 'This
relates to a prime suspect in relation to involvement in the murder of
Detective Garda McCabe. He is working for a state funded agency
and APSO has notified the Gardaí that the individual is moving
between different locations.' Deputy Higgins demanded to know
what steps were being taken to ensure that the Gardaí would be
afforded the opportunity of interviewing the individual and bringing
charges if necessary.

The statement from the APSO chief executive had also pointed
out that before his 1991 departure to Central America, Damery had
been required by the government of El Salvador to obtain a police
certificate of character. The statement added, 'The [Garda] Crime
and Security Branch in Phoenix Park provided that certificate and
confirmed that he had no criminal record.'

While a certificate of character is issued from Garda headquarters,
it is confirmed that the Garda procedures involved are carried out at
the local Garda division of the applicant. It is also confirmed that the
procedures normally include taking of fingerprints for purposes of
identification in the event that the applicant might come to grief in an
overseas jurisdiction.

In the first half of the 1990s Damery was working in El Salvador.
He was part of a group of Irish volunteer workers, among whom was
Niall Connolly, also on assignment under the aegis of APSO. They
were then involved in the development of a new town. Established
and populated by refugees returning from Honduras at the end of civil
war in El Salvador, the town, called Segundo Montes, was regarded as
a new model for the country. It had strong links with Ireland due to
the support and activities of the Irish El Salvador Support
Committee.

But Damery and Connolly were expelled from Segundo Montes amid allegations of political bias and an attempted takeover of the town which soured relations between the town and its Irish support and aid agencies.

Following questions in the Dáil at the end of 1996 when it emerged that Damery was wanted for questioning in connection with the Adare murder investigation, it was revealed that he was then in Nicaragua. It would subsequently be revealed by APSO that Damery's contract with the agency extended to 1999.

In August 2001, Damery's onetime colleague in El Salvador, Niall Connolly, was one of the three Irishmen arrested at Bogota Airport in Columbia where they would become known as 'The Columbia Three'.

Detained with Connolly were Martin McCauley, originally from Lurgan in county Armagh, and James Monaghan from Rathmullen in county Donegal, both of whom had strong links to the republican movement and had served in positions in the Sinn Féin party structure. McCauley had figured in one of the great controversies of the northern conflict. He and a younger companion, Michael Tighe, were in a barn which was under surveillance and also electronically bugged when they came under fire from the security services. Tighe was killed and McCauley wounded. Both had been unarmed. The circumstances of the shooting became part of the 'shoot to kill' investigation headed by John Stalker, who was then the rising star of the British police force. But, in a long-running stand off with the RUC and its Chief Constable, Jack Harmon, the tape that may have recorded what went on in the barn was never recovered. On returning to his Manchester base, Stalker was at the centre of corruption allegations that he and his defenders branded a smear campaign. He subsequently resigned from the force.

McCauley had received a suspended sentence for possession of a firearm in 1985 and, over the next decade, was prominent in Sinn Féin election campaigns. James Monaghan had twice been jailed for IRA activities during the 1970s and, after his release in 1985, became a member of the Ard Comhairle of the Sinn Féin party. From 1999 he had been associated with an organisation working to integrate ex-prisoners back into society which had been set up as part of the multi-faceted strands of the Good Friday Agreement.

All three of the men were in Columbia on forged passports. Accused of working with the FARC guerilla movement, they claimed initially to be journalists and later that they had come to Columbia to study the peace process and the ecology of the country.

Niall Connolly claimed that he was the Sinn Féin representative since 1996 in Cuba where he lived with his partner and two children.

But in echoes of the immediate aftermath of the Adare shooting when the IRA and Sinn Féin disowned those involved, the Sinn Féin President, Gerry Adams, initially denied that Connolly was a representative of the party. 'Efforts to make Sinn Féin accountable for these three Irishmen are totally unjustified,' the Sinn Féin leader stated, much in the same vein as his initial Adare statement when he claimed that linkage of the IRA to the killing was 'mischief making' by political opponents of his party.

But then a Cuban government spokesman stated, 'Mr Niall Terence Connolly is the official representative of Sinn Féin for Cuba and Latin America,' and the Sinn Féin stance changed, much as it did in the Adare case.

Mr Adams discovered that Connolly was an official party appointment. But even when he was enlightened, Mr Adams said that Connolly's appointment had been made 'without the knowledge or authorisation of the international department or any other party structure, including the party chairman and myself'. He somehow managed to explain how the party hierarchy could be oblivious of the existence of their man in Havana. Adams said that Connolly had been asked to work for Sinn Féin by a senior party member acting independently. Again, that sounded very much like the IRA Army Council statement a week after the Adare shooting when the killers were recognised as IRA volunteers and the *Late Late Show* statement from Mr Adams in 2004 when he contended that the authorisation for the Adare operation had somehow come from 'a lower rank'.

In the year of his Bogota arrest, Niall Connolly had been engaged as an interpreter and guide for an Irish television crew making a documentary about the Cuban health service. In the advance preparation involved, the television team contacted the Irish Embassy in Mexico for assistance in finding a person who had command of both English and Spanish and preferably somebody who was familiar with the setup in Cuba. The Irish embassy identified Niall Connolly as a suitable candidate and he was engaged for the location filming in Cuba in mid 2001.

So, Niall Connolly was known to the Irish diplomatic service. That might not be surprising as he had worked with APSO which came under the Department of Foreign Affairs. But the Mexico embassy knew of him and knew he was in Cuba. The Cuban authorities knew him. But for some reason the president, chairman and relevant bodies within Sinn Féin would plead ignorance, not only of appointing him as their representative for Cuba and Latin America, but of having any party connection to him or knowledge of his status as the party's overseas representative.

However, following in much the same pattern as the Adare case, having disowned and repudiated those in the spotlight of suspicion, Sinn Féin would wait for the dust to settle and then lend its influence and campaigning experience to the sustained efforts to have the accused freed.

While Paul Damery remained out of reach in Nicaragua, a second man on the Garda wanted list had absconded to mainland Europe. As the Adare trial had heard, fingerprints had been recovered from the getaway car which pointed the Garda investigation in the direction of Gerry Roche. A former activist with the Irish Republican Socialist Party and its Irish National Liberation Army military wing he switched allegiance to the IRA in the early 1980s. He lived in Shannon and was under round the clock surveillance by the Special Branch and had been spotted leaving Shannon on the eve of the Adare shooting. He did not return to his home and partner.

Besides the two wanted men who were outside the jurisdiction, the Adare investigation and hunt for the wider team involved in the crime produced a valuable return in intelligence information as well as flushing out subversives.

The general public revulsion and, in other cases, scruples and remorse in the wake of the brutal and cold-blooded killing in Adare triggered more than a backlash against the IRA and its Sinn Féin mouthpieces who could not be described as apologists, as no apology for the atrocity was forthcoming.

Whatever advances in political respectability had been gained by Sinn Féin over the 17 months of the break in IRA military action were shattered by the 15 Kalashnikov bullets that tore into the powerless detectives as they sat in a disoriented state in the aftershock of their car being rammed by a jeep.

Within days of the Adare shooting, an informant pointed Gardaí to the location of a secret bomb-making factory in the midlands. In the raid on a farmhouse at Clonaslee, county Laois, bombs and bomb-making materials were found in a bunker beneath the farmhouse and in an outhouse. Seized were 16 mortar bombs and 60 kilograms of Semtex, equal to almost ten stones of the plastic explosive which had been brought into the country in tens of tons during the massive, mid-1980s IRA importation from Libya of arms. The security forces reckoned that the bomb-making bunker was one of around five that the IRA was operating at any one time.

In the course of what turned into a marathon investigation and manhunt that ran for almost two years before the five who went on trial in 1999 were held and charged.

When John Carroll, a leading Sinn Féin figure in the midlands, appeared before the Special Criminal Court in mid-1998, the charge he pleaded guilty to was of membership of the IRA on the date immediately before the Adare killing took place, 7 June 1996.

He had been interviewed on many occasions after his arrest in July 1997 by the Adare murder investigators, led by Detective Inspector John Kerin.

During one interview, he made a statement in which he admitted that he had been a member of the IRA but had severed his connections since the day of the Adare shooting.

Aged 47 when he pleaded guilty before the Special Criminal Court in July 1998, Carroll had been sentenced by the same court in 1976 for armed robbery and possession of firearms. Then he had also received a concurrent 12-month sentence for IRA membership. He served six years of an eight-year sentence.

A farmer and father of two living at The Ring, Crinkle, outside Birr in county Offaly, Carroll was a Sinn Féin member of Birr Urban Council but had resigned his party membership and continued to serve as an independent member of the local authority.

After the Adare killing, Councillor Carroll had a letter published in his local newspaper in which he announced his resignation from Sinn Féin.

In the Special Criminal Court in July 1998, Carroll said in evidence, 'I made a decision and made it public that I would have no association with anything of a subversive nature in the future.' He told the court that subversive individuals were outside his 'circle of friends' since he made the decision to resign from Sinn Féin.

Councillor Carroll, who in the 2004 local elections held his Birr council seat and also won election to Offaly County Council, had also given a sworn undertaking in court not to associate with subversive organisations or individuals.

While Carroll had been arrested during the Adare investigation, the prosecuting barrister said that there was no suggestion that there was any link between Carroll and the events in Adare. In his testimony, the leader of the Adare murder hunt, Detective Inspector John Kerin, stated that Gardaí had no evidence to suggest that Carroll had been involved with subversives since July of the previous year.

Having taken into consideration Councillor Carroll's plea of guilty to IRA membership and his undertaking not to associate with subversives, Mr Justice Frederick Morris sentenced him to five years in prison which was suspended on his own bond to be of good behaviour for five years.

In the same week in July 1998, another former IRA man from the midlands who had cut his links with the organisation after the Adare crime, also appeared before the Special Criminal Court.

Michael Ward, then 31 and a father of two, living at Clononeen, Borris-in-Ossory in county Laois, pleaded guilty to IRA membership in the period up to a week after the death of Detective McCabe.

He told the court, 'My regrets are that a member of the Gardaí died because of my involvement in an illegal organisation. But I had no hand, act or part in that death.'

Also detained during the widespread investigation into subversives and their activities, Detective Inspector Kerin gave evidence that Ward had been interviewed on eight different occasions. While Gardaí had found nothing to connect him to the IRA during a search of his home in July 1997, he had made a statement admitting IRA membership.

The statement said, 'I am a member of the IRA for a number of years. I condemn the shooting of Detective Garda McCabe in Adare. I did not have any contact with the IRA or persons connected with them since. I honestly did not know anything about the Garda murder.'

Ward, who pleaded to membership of the IRA on 13 June 1996, was said by Detective Inspector Kerin to have no previous convictions and came from a good family.

Mr Justice Frederick Morris sentenced Ward to three years in prison which the court suspended in view of his guilty plea and previous good record. The sentence was suspended on condition that Ward would not associate with subversive organisations or their personnel.

Chapter 16

'In a secret way.' That was the clue that former US President, Bill Clinton, let slip in an uncharacteristically unguarded moment during a *Prime Time* RTÉ interview.

The intuitive sure-footedness in world diplomacy, discussion, debate and normal exchanges that had made him 'the great communicator' deserted him briefly. He paused at that moment, not so much to choose his words but to remind himself mentally of what was already known and what was known only by those who had a place at the most inner of inner circles. Though it was not picked up by interviewer, Miriam O'Callaghan, or in follow-up coverage by the rest of the media, in this case the IRA would not have been thanking Bill Clinton.

It was mid-July 2004 and the northern peace process had moved into a phase that held out a promise of permanent peace. Questioned about the peace process and the obstinate stance of the IRA against decommissioning demands from the Ulster unionists, President Clinton was prompted to balance his remarks. While he felt the IRA was 'too hung up' on the possible interpretation of decommissioning as 'surrender', he paused to pick out a positive example. He then went on to say that the IRA had contributed positively to the process 'when they participated or helped, at least in a secret way, in trying to make sure that the Real IRA would never repeat Omagh'.

'Secret ways' are an integral part of every conflict since time immemorial and may, as in the case of the Cold War that hatched so many tales of betrayal and counter-betrayal both factual and fictional, assume a virtual war-footing stance in times of standoff or peace. That intelligence gathering and surveillance continued during the northern peace process was one of the key objections of the hawkish elements in the republican movement who felt that their membership and methods were being flushed out under cover of peace. Intelligence

Special day – out of uniform and into plain clothes. Jerry McCabe's first day as a Special Branch detective, 21 November 1972.

Garda 15860G Jerry McCabe at his Templemore passing out parade with his father Johnny.

Ann and Jerry on their wedding day, 21 September 1967.

Lively social life – Ann and Jerry at a dinner dance in 1968.

A place in the sun – a holiday snap from Spain early in their marriage.

On duty at home – Jerry snatches a rest after a family meal.

In the presence of his Grace – good-humoured Jerry McCabe plays the straight man to funny man and long-time family friend, Brendan Grace.

Jerry McCabe as he is best remembered in his adopted Limerick – smartly turned out.

Ann and Jerry at a close friend's wedding.

Partners – Jerry sharing his 50th birthday party celebrations
with partner and friend, Ben O'Sullivan.

The McCabe family: (left to right) Ross, Jerry, Ian, Ann, Stacey, Mark and John.

Grad Dad – Jerry at the secondary school graduation of only daughter, Stacey.

Spanning three generations of McCabes but with Jerry missed:
Ann, Ross and Jerry's father, Johnny.

Fond memories – remembering Jerry with a smile.
Ann McCabe and father-in-law, Johnny.

US honour – Ann at the launch of the Jerry McCabe Memorial Exchange
Fellowship between the US and Ireland.

Family grief – Ann and daughter Stacey at a memorial to the assassinated
President John F Kennedy with Jean Kennedy Smith (middle).

gathering, but by whom and who it was directed at, also became one of the most convoluted and deadly causes of breakdown for the Northern Executive.

Through 'supergrass' trials in Northern Ireland, as well as disclosures and confessions by former operatives in the clandestine services and within the ranks of paramilitaries, the public caught fleeting and probably false trail glimpses of the shadowy world of informers and those who practice the intelligence craft. Like the secret world opened up in the novels of John Le Carré, it was the murky alien world of a treacherous trade with blandishments and blackmail the most common means of recruitment. But the most valued and sought after informer was the double agent or mole. Besides inducements or threats of exposure, moles could also be won over when the authorities either took a soft line or waived prosecution and likely jail sentences. However, the higher the value of the flow of information from a mole or double agent, the higher the price to be paid. Not the price in terms of the fiscal reward, but in the tightrope walking risk to the mole's life and also in terms of the lives and sacrifice of others. When it came to weighing up the importance of a mole or adversary who had been 'turned', it has emerged that the security and intelligence authorities were prepared to allow crimes and killings to take place that could have been prevented, but only at the cost of unmasking the informer. The choices made were to keep the informer in place, the flow of information preserved and to allow events take their oftentimes deadly course, without intervention.

Intelligence gathering, informants and informers were then a natural, if not routine, element of the everyday battle of wits that went on in the Republic and in the region around Limerick between the forces of law and subversives. Gathering of information and dissemination of information and disinformation was a two-way process. This clearly emerged in the trial of the Adare killers and in matters that came before the courts in previous years.

The darkly forbidding, brown-brick Garda headquarters that then dominated Limerick city's Henry Street was the setting for a national sensation when it emerged, in September 1991, that the IRA had a spy at the heart of the local police force. This spy was not only stationed in the regional nerve centre, but also had access to its communications centre and its national and international pool of information.

The spy was a 28 year old Garda, Denis Kelly, one of two brothers serving in the force who, in his nine years as a Garda, had received four Garda Commissioner commendations. A bachelor from Cullen in the Mallow area of county Cork, he was caught redhanded in an elaborate sting operation. Two weeks before he appeared before the Special Criminal Court, he pleaded guilty to a charge under the Official Secrets Act.

With compelling suspicions of an 'inside' leak of information to the IRA and the local active service unit especially, the spy was trapped through the use of bogus information and deployment of undercover Gardaí.

Set up from national level, detailed planning had gone into the transmission of false information and to the covert surveillance that would track that same information being passed on.

On 27 September 1991, Garda Kelly was on duty at the communications centre in Henry Street when a fax message came through from Detective Superintendent Kevin Carty of the Garda Security Section which was directed to Inspector Tony Fennessy. The 'top secret' message concerned Provisional IRA arms dumps and training camps at three locations in the Limerick and Tipperary areas. The instruction to Inspector Fennessy was to prepare to swoop on the dumps.

The spy Garda took notes from the fax and made two phone calls from the station to persons who the Gardaí believed were members of the IRA.

When he finished his duty shift at 2.00 p.m., Garda Kelly was shadowed to Cecil Street where there was a public phone box located on the footpath. In the phone box, the Garda received a call from his IRA contact and was heard giving details of the three locations of the suspected arms dumps. When arrested he said, 'It's all over. It had to come to an end sometime.'

When he appeared in the Special Criminal Court at the end of January 1992, the prosecuting Detective Superintendent, James McHugh, said that Kelly had denied being sympathetic to the IRA, but that he had been blackmailed and had passed on information because of a drink problem.

While the superintendent told the court that Kelly had substantial financial problems and did have a drink problem in the past, Kelly stated to the investigating Gardaí that he had intended to trade information in return for information on importation of drugs into Limerick. The superintendent commented to the court, 'I think that would be bizarre in the extreme. I would find it very difficult to accept that as an explanation.' He added that Kelly was 'remorseful, not just for his own part, but for his family and colleagues'.

When sentencing Kelly to five years in jail, Mr Justice Frederick Morris stated, 'One cannot ignore the gravity of this offence. The importance of preserving the confidentiality of Garda information is something that must be recognised.' Passing of information to subversives 'strikes at the very heart of society' and could not be tolerated, the judge said.

In comparison to the tactics and undercover work that netted the spy in the Garda headquarters, the bulk of the intelligence gathering by general members of the Garda force in addition to Special Branch detectives is more often than not tedious, and often has no special value or significance. Yet, it was everyday detection and routine compiling of potentially useful information that helped in bringing the case against the Adare killers and others.

On the seventh day of the trial, a 'trial within a trial' took place as the barristers and legal teams for the accused challenged the use, as evidence, of video recordings that helped two witnesses in identification of two of the main IRA men.

Special Branch detectives regularly took still pictures as well as video recordings of republican activities, including funerals, commemorations and demonstrations, and also gathered pictorial evidence of goings and comings at meetings including the Sinn Féin Ard Fheis. Special Branch men and women, in casual dress, would take up positions outside Sinn Féin conferences and other assemblies to take note of people they recognised, and especially of new faces. Using electronic surveillance, detectives were able to identify faces not previously recognisable.

It was video recordings of persons attending or partaking in republican events that were used by the Adare investigation team. The videos were shown to two witnesses who had passed through Adare some time before the raid and had seen one man sitting on a wall and another at the wheel of a silver car. The use of the recordings in a compilation video was challenged by the legal teams representing Kevin Walsh and Jeremiah Sheehy. But the ruling of the judges of the Special Criminal Court was to allow the evidence.

The recordings had been made at: the Bodenstown republican commemoration in 1993; a funeral in March 1995; a Sean Sabhat (South) commemoration in Limerick; a parade in Limerick during 1996; as well as Easter commemorations in Nenagh, county Tipperary, in the same year.

During the cross-examination when one of the Garda witnesses involved said that he had edited out sections of the video that showed paramilitary trappings, uniforms, flags and emblems, the barrister for the defence pointed out that the tricolour had been left in. It was left to Mr Justice Johnson to point out to the barrister that the tricolour was not subversive.

The bachelor farmer who had provided refuge in his secluded property at Toomevara for the IRA men who fled from Adare after the killing, also came to the attention of Gardaí through routine observation by a Garda. Patrick Harty was in his early fifties when he declined to give evidence for the state prosecution, and was said by his solicitor to be a person with a sense of loyalty to the past and also a religious man. As his legal representative told the court, Harty had not come to the attention of the Gardaí before and his only offences had related to parking fines in Limerick and Kilkenny. But a Garda had seen and recognised Harty during night-time activity when he was putting up posters promoting the republican priest, Fr Patrick Ryan, who contested a European Parliament election in the Munster constituency.

An integral part of Garda life throughout all periods of unrest and subversive activities has been 'border duty', when members of the force were assigned to border counties in the Republic. But, in addition to everyday policing, detectives and others engaged along the border would also be involved in identifying and checking out buildings, outhouses and apparently abandoned or vacant houses that could possibly be used as a place of refuge for subversives. During border duty too, Gardaí would work on establishing contacts and potential sources of information. All that activity was co-ordinated to maintain a body of intelligence that was constantly updated.

It was intelligence work which led to the eventual capture of the heavily disguised Kevin Walsh, the most hunted criminal in the country, when a large force of Gardaí surrounded the farmhouse in Cavan where the IRA man had laid low for eight months.

It was not until 18 months after the trial of the Adare killers that the farmer who provided the safe house for Walsh was himself brought before the Special Criminal Court. There it would be disclosed that he had admitted to concealment of weapons on his property and had identified the hiding places to Gardaí.

John Carolan, a father of six from Greagh na Darragh, Mullagh, pleaded guilty to having guns and mortar components in 1998 when he was brought before the Special Criminal Court.

The court was told by Garda Superintendent Tadhg Foley that the confession about the guns and other items was made during questioning in connection with a different investigation.

The farmer showed Gardaí where six Luger pistols were hidden in the roof of his dairy, and also pointed out fields belonging to neighbours where barrels containing a Kalashnikov rifle and mortar components were buried.

Like Patrick Harty in Toomevara, the then 57 year old Carolan had not previously come to the attention of the Gardaí.

While the prosecuting Garda superintendent said that the farmer had been helpful to the investigation, Mr Justice Frederick Morris observed that there had been no expression of regret and no undertaking to disassociate himself from any organisation by Carolan, who he jailed for four years.

Chapter 17

The double speak from both the Provisional IRA and the Sinn Féin party leadership began within hours of the slaying of Jerry McCabe and continued in various forms in the intervening ten years.

Jerry McCabe died of automatic gunshot wounds through the back in the minutes around 7.00 a.m. As the Special Criminal Court would be told by Detective Garda Patrick Kelly who was one of the first called in to bolster the investigation, within hours of the crime the investigation centred on the IRA gang based in Patrickswell outside Limerick city.

On the same black Friday, the IRA issued a categorical denial which was backed up by a statement from Gerry Adams, in which he accused other interests of seeking to damage the republican movement by pointing the finger at the IRA.

The IRA statement was not an unattributed leak, nor from the confidential sources that regularly characterised the IRA propaganda methods when heading off trouble with damage limitation tactics. The statement was officially authenticated with the traditional signature of 'P O'Neill'. The statement was issued through the Irish Republican Publicity Bureau in Dublin and as such got the full treatment from *An Phoblacht/Republican News*. In its issue of 13 June 1996, six days after the killing, the republican weekly published a top of the page report with the strap line *IRA Denies Involvement in Limerick Shooting* and under the headline *Sinn Féin Repudiates Killing of Garda*.

The report stated:

> *The killing of Special Branch man Gerard [sic] McCabe and the wounding of another in an armed raid in Adare on June 7 was not the work of the IRA, according to a statement issued by them on the same day.*

'None of our volunteers or units were in any way involved in this morning's incident at Adare. There was absolutely no IRA involvement,' said a statement which was signed P O'Neill, Republican Publicity Bureau, Dublin.

On Tuesday, 11 June, Sinn Féin President Gerry Adams responded to the continuing speculation around the killing of McCabe.

'Despite the repudiation by the Sinn Féin leadership of the killing of McCabe and wounding of Garda O'Sullivan at Adare, and despite our public expression of regret and condolences to the families of the two Gardaí, there has been a continuing political effort to link the killing with Sinn Féin's efforts to restore the peace process. 'This is clearly deliberate mischief making and is aimed at undermining Sinn Féin's role in the search for peace.

'Let me reiterate Sinn Féin's attitude. We extend our sincerest condolences to the families of the two garda. It is clear that the killing in Adare can form no part of the republican struggle. On the contrary, actions such as this would be a dis-service to the struggle.

'Those who are trying to use this killing to undermine Sinn Féin know this. In fact this is their political agenda. The IRA last Friday said that none of its volunteers or units were involved in the Adare incident. I accept that position.'

But the story had changed utterly by the next edition of *An Phoblacht/Republican News* which carried another IRA official statement, but on this occasion there was no mention of endorsement of the credibility of the IRA statement from the Sinn Féin President.

In its issue of 20 June, the publication included a boxed panel at the top of page four headlined *Adare Contravened Army Orders – IRA*, and in prominent display, the report underneath stated:

On Friday, 14 June, the Irish Republican Army issued a second statement clarifying the situation in relation to the shooting incident in Adare when a garda was killed.

The 14 June statement reads:

'On Friday last [June 7], the IRA leadership issued a statement regarding the killing of Garda Jerry McCabe and the wounding of Garda Ben O'Sullivan at Adare.

'We did so in the firm knowledge that standing army orders recently reiterated to units, expressly prohibit any volunteer from taking 'any military action against 26-county forces under any circumstances whatsoever' and in the knowledge that no operations had been cleared by the leadership.

'Our initial investigations have established however that individual volunteers were party to what happened at Adare. In light of that we wish to clarify our position.

'The shootings at Adare were in direct contravention of standing IRA army orders. Such shootings were not, nor cannot be, sanctioned by the Army leadership.

'Those who carried out these shootings did so to the detriment of the Republican cause. We wish to make clear that we disavow these actions and will not tolerate any activity which is damaging to our struggle.

'In conclusion let us send our condolences to the families who have suffered as a result of these shootings.

P O'Neill'

On the same page, and below the panel displaying the IRA's statement clarifying its position, there was a report under the by-line of Anton Ó Mordha headlined *Fears Raised Over Garda Abuse of Detainees.*

The report's opening paragraph stated, 'Solicitors acting on behalf of John Quinn have expressed concern about his treatment while in custody as a Garda inquiry into injuries sustained by Jeremiah Sheehy in custody continues.'

The article reported that the Irish Council for Civil Liberties and the Independent TD Tony Gregory had expressed concern. Reporting that eight of 18 arrested in the investigation were women, the report went on, 'The Gardaí seem to have targeted wives and partners of men they have questioned and, in the case of John and Connie Quinn, their mother Ann.'

The report explained that John Quinn's mother had been arrested during a visit to Henry Street Garda station where her son was being held and that she had been released later. The report said that Geraldine McNamara from Tipperary, and her husband Bobby, had been abused when they were arrested and detained. It was also recorded that the Department of Justice had issued a statement that acknowledged that Jeremiah Sheehy sustained injuries while in custody.

In the edition of the following week, *An Phoblacht/Republican News* carried a report headlined *Further Evidence of Garda Abuse in Limerick.*

That article, under the by-line of Liam Ó Coileain, dated July 11, stated that 'in some of the worst abuses, both men and women are too intimidated to speak publicly to the media'.

The report quoted Noel Kavanagh from Ballyfermot, Dublin, of being arrested at 7.00 a.m. on 26 June and taken to Limerick where he was held for 48 hours. He said he had been beaten while in custody by a Special Branch detective based in Dublin. The report also stated that Tom Maxwell from Mullingar had been arrested just before 7.00 a.m. on 28 June and also taken to Henry Street Garda headquarters in Limerick city.

While the official statement of 14 June claimed to 'clarify' the IRA's position, it tended to confuse and to raise many questions which have reverberated through the decade since the Adare shooting, which IRA statements termed 'an incident'.

As in all previous occasions when Gardaí or members of the armed forces were killed or came under fire from subversives, the IRA trotted out its line about what became familiar as Standing Order 8 from the IRA Army Council which specifically ruled out any military action against the security and law enforcement forces in the Republic. While the prohibition was routinely fed to the media, in the dozen or more cases in which Gardaí and members of the army were killed, wounded, maimed or came under attack, there was never any suggestion of disciplinary action against those who contravened the standing orders of the Irish Republican Army. No IRA active service unit or volunteer could have been under any misapprehension as the IRA statement of 14 June pointed out that the order expressly ruling out action against forces of the Republic had 'recently been reiterated' to units. The reiteration of standing orders is likely to have been issued with the February 1996 resumption of the armed struggle, after a pause of almost 18 months in IRA action in the northern conflict.

In the ambiguous terminology that crops up most regularly in military and political public statements when a cleaning up operation is underway, the IRA states the obvious but, in other instances, evades specifics.

While setting out the standing orders prohibition, the statement says of the events that occurred in Adare, 'Such shootings were not, nor cannot, be sanctioned by the Army leadership.' What seems to have been lost on whoever drafted the statement was that if the standing orders to the IRA from its Army Council expressly prohibited attacks on the security forces of the Republic, there would therefore be no question whatsoever of the Army leadership sanctioning such actions, as that would be in direct contravention of its own standing orders.

In disavowing the Adare actions and stating that the IRA would not tolerate any activity that damaged the republican struggle, the statement clearly indicates that the IRA members involved at Adare were acting independently.

Yet, once they were arrested and detained, the Adare gang that had been disowned and their actions disavowed by the IRA would get the fullest and most tenacious support from Sinn Féin and the IRA in fighting against their imprisonment for the crime.

But the Sinn Féin campaign on behalf of the Adare killers would also revive nagging questions and controversy. The Adare questions that would not go away would elicit answers in later years that were not at all in line with what the IRA stated in the wake of its investigation in June 1996.

In 2004, when pressed by *Late Late Show* host Pat Kenny on the question of whether the Adare action had been sanctioned by the IRA, Gerry Adams stated that the approval had emanated from 'a low rank'.

Was the Sinn Féin President seriously suggesting that an IRA cadre, led by a seasoned gunman who was of senior stature and commanded respect at the highest levels in the organisation, would be prepared to accept orders from a figure of low rank?

It seemed to have escaped the Sinn Féin President that back in June 1996 the IRA leadership said in an official statement that not only had the Adare raid not been sanctioned by the Irish Republican Army leadership, but the IRA men involved had been acting independently. If that was the case, how could the action have been approved from any quarter or rank? Furthermore, how low in the IRA structure could an operation like Adare (with assault rifles and other equipment, as well as stolen cars, moved around the country) have been going ahead without the knowledge of the IRA leadership?

An answer that was markedly different was given when Pat Kenny posed the same question to the daughter of the Sinn Féin President's constant companion in photo opportunities, the self-professed former IRA volunteer, convicted gunrunner and member of the Dáil since 2002, Martin Ferris.

Having been elected to her father's Kerry County Council seat, Toireasa Ferris was a guest on the *Late Late Show* in early 2005. She was interviewed before the biggest television audience in the land when she appeared in her capacity as Mayor of Kerry.

With her replies, Toireasa Ferris stirred new controversy and prompted an abortive effort by local political opponents to unseat her as Mayor of Kerry.

She was firm in her refusal to condemn the killing of her fellow Kerry native, Detective Jerry McCabe, and stated that the IRA men involved at Adare had been 'fundraising'.

The question then arises: fundraising for who or what?

If, as the official statement of the time insisted, the operation at Adare had been carried out by IRA volunteers acting independently, and had not been sanctioned or approved by the IRA leadership, what purpose was the attempted robbery mounted for, and what or who was it to benefit?

But other more serious questions arise and remain clouded in some mystery.

Members of the Adare gang were armed to the teeth. Two Kalashnikov automatic assault rifles, a shotgun and a pistol were carried. At least two vehicles had been stolen in Dublin and delivered to a rendezvous point outside Limerick city on the eve of the planned robbery.

In IRA operations, volunteers are given orders and the weapons, vehicles and equipment required for the operation are routed to them from varying sources through couriers.

Consequently, in the case of Adare, the arms used in the raid had been delivered to the area. In the same way, the weapons had to be collected and taken out of the area for storage in what was regarded as a safe place.

The IRA statement, which set out to 'clarify' its position after its investigation which had turned its initial statement on its head, was issued on 14 June, a Friday. While then acknowledging that those involved in the Adare shooting were IRA members, the statement persisted in denying any foreknowledge of the raid.

Yet less than 24 hours after the IRA issued its first official statement that categorically denied IRA involvement, the IRA was taking action.

An IRA member based in the midlands received a telephone call and instructions to go to the farm in Toomevara and to check out if the five members of the IRA gang were still in hiding there. The man made his way to the farm where he established that the men had left. That was on Saturday, 8 June, just one day after the Adare killing. So, instructions were being given to IRA men in the Republic that the IRA leadership would say they knew nothing about at the time.

Less than a week later the IRA man in the midlands received further instructions. He was detailed to return to the Toomevara farm. There he recovered the weapons which had been supplied for the Adare operation and conveyed the arms to a pick-up place. The guns were recovered, by a person unknown to him, at a later date.

The recovery of the arms took place on the Thursday after the killing of Jerry McCabe. The date was 13 June. Yet on 14 June, a day after the orders had been issued and carried out in removing the Adare weapons, the IRA issued its second official statement which denied that its leadership had given the go ahead for the atrocity that unfolded in Adare.

Chapter 18

In a Dáil chamber that seethed with anger most clearly voiced by opposition spokesmen, the Sinn Féin Deputy, Caoimhghin Ó Caoláin, appeared to be preoccupied with other matters.

In the formal and studied statement required of him, the Minister for Justice, John O'Donoghue, spoke of the 'savagery and inhumanity' of the 'merciless' killing in Adare. The speakers from the main opposition party benches were not tempering their words. Whatever deal had been hatched in the Special Criminal Court, it was 'murder, murder, murder' the Dáil heard.

The rage was given voice in the emergency debate that had been slated for the earliest resumption of the Dáil on the Tuesday after the abrupt ending of the trial. Outcry and fury had reverberated over the weekend from all quarters. Except for Sinn Féin. Even before the presiding judge had passed sentence, that party's leaders had stepped up the campaign to get the Adare killers out of jail.

In his brief contribution to the debate of Tuesday, 9 February 1999, Deputy Ó Caoláin made a passing reference to what he described as 'an appalling event'. But, under a barrage of calls for condemnation of the killing from other party benches, he concentrated his attention on charges of ill-treatment in custody of the jailed killers.

It was possibly this concern that the law of the land should protect the human and constitutional rights of any accused person that caused him and his party to miss what was one of the most important passages in the contribution of the Minister for Justice.

Minister John O'Donoghue explained to the Dáil that the early release of prisoners under the British-Irish Agreement was not a straightforward matter of unlocking the doors for those who claimed that their offences were 'political'. Neither was it the case that those convicted of terrorist offences automatically qualified for early release.

The Minister took some pains in the question and answer exchanges to detail to the Dáil that eligibility for early release depended on his say so.

Following the signing of the British-Irish Agreement, the Minister explained, there had been substantial legislation dealing with the Commission on the Release of Prisoners.

'That legislation specifies quite clearly that the question of the Commission advising on the release of prisoners is precisely that, an advisory role.'

'They do not have the power to direct the Minister of the day to release a prisoner,' the Minister said.

The key decision then was not a matter of who qualified for early release but who was nominated to the Commission by the Minister. Because the powers of early release were reserved to the Minister for Justice, he also made the point that even in cases where the Minister of the day referred prisoners to the Commission, the minister still had the option of accepting or not accepting the advice of the Commission.

'It is clearly the wish of the democratically elected representatives of the people of this country that those who were convicted of this atrocity should serve their sentences.'

The Minister set down even stronger commitments to the Dáil.

'I believe that no Minister for Justice would, or indeed could, find acceptance for a position whereby he would release these people under the British-Irish Agreement,' he declared.

Reiterating that it was a matter for the Minister for Justice of the day to refer the names for early release to the Commission, he stated, 'I will not be referring those names to the Commission.'

Minister O'Donoghue went even further. 'I do not believe that any successor to this office will refer those people to the Commission. Moreover it was clearly understood during the negotiations on this agreement what the position was.'

His words of reassurance to the Dáil were, 'I do not believe there is any need for any member to cause, however unintentionally, the slightest worry to the family of the late Detective Garda McCabe.'

The Minister also invoked the authority and endorsement of the Taoiseach, Bertie Ahern, as reinforcement of his Dáil pledges on the possibility of early release.

That the government had been preparing for the trial and the continued calls for the early release mechanism to be activated, was made plain. 'I have had numerous discussions with the Taoiseach in relation to this case, long before it arrived in the Special Criminal Court, in the context of the early release provisions of the agreement. He made it very clear to me at all times that the people who were convicted of this offence would not qualify for early release under the terms of the agreement.'

The Minister also read into the record of the Dáil his previous commitment on the Adare case during the debate on the amendment to the constitution legislation on 21 April 1998.

His statement to the Dáil on that occasion also knitted the name of the Taoiseach into the commitment on early release.

The Minister had then stated:

> *While emphasising that I will not speculate about the implications of the agreement for individual cases, it is right that I should comment on one case, that is the case of those facing charges arising from the murder of Detective Garda Jerry McCabe which has been the subject of recent media speculation. While obviously it would be inappropriate for me to comment in detail on any case pending before the courts, the government has made clear in its contacts with all groups its views that persons who may be convicted in connection with this murder will not come within the ambit of the agreement.*

The Minister added in 1998:

> *I cannot put it any further than that. I have given the assurance on numerous occasions and so has the Taoiseach. This matter was raised during the negotiations which led to the British-Irish Agreement and it was made clear by officials from my department that those who were convicted of this atrocity would not qualify under the early release provisions of the British-Irish Agreement.*

But the solemn pledge made to the Dáil by the Minister on his own behalf and those who came after him as holder of the justice portfolio fell on deaf ears in the republican movement.

Sinn Féin, from its highest levels, was pressing for the release of the Adare killers before they actually went on trial. For some extraordinary reasons, there was not one protest from any quarter that a campaign to have prisoners released, even before their cases were tried and verdicts handed down, was anticipating the judgement of the Special Criminal Court and could be called into question. Normal conventions also were absent in the conduct of Sinn Féin when Gerry Adams and chief negotiator, Martin McGuinness, went on local and national radio to proclaim the right of the Adare gang to early release hours before the judges of the Special Criminal Court handed down the sentences on the charges that the gang had pleaded guilty to.

Their campaign was unremitting and the pressure for release of the IRA men was applied at every available opportunity. Instead of the peace and grieving time that they had appealed for at the end of what was a trial for them also, the widow and the McCabe family found themselves buffeted and their everyday lives upset and disturbed like fragile objects at the centre of a cyclone. They could sense the storm gathering and the rumblings that preceded it. Then came sharp cracks of lightning and frightening flashes followed by the booming menace of the storm at its height. Ann McCabe and her family experienced month after month of media pressure as Sinn Féin and their allies chipped relentlessly away at the government position on the early release of the Adare killers. Each time the issue cropped up, the press would lay siege to Ann's private telephone and home.

What was she to say? What could she say? While the efforts to undermine government resolve went on relentlessly, the person who had been a private wife and mother up to June 1996 was being represented as an obstacle to the peace process and questioned on why she should deny the peoples of the Republic and the North the chance of an end to conflict. It was not just the government that came under pressure. And worst of all for the McCabes, each media storm that whipped itself up and eventually blew itself out was always followed by another. There seemed to be no end.

The Adare trial concluded in early February 1999. But the demands for early release were being voiced in public by May of that year. At the Sinn Féin Ard Fheis, an IRA prisoner on early release from Portlaoise Jail was the front man for the demands. In this instance, Patrick Kelly relayed support for the party leadership and the early release campaign on behalf of IRA prisoners in the country's top security prison. His call for the early release of the five who had pleaded guilty to the manslaughter of a detective Garda was loudly cheered by Sinn Féin delegates. He accused the Taoiseach, Bertie Ahern, of backtracking on the early release issue and contended that the government had buckled under pressure from the Garda Representative Association.

At that same Sinn Féin party congress where the northern peace process and the concessions demanded from the republican movement dominated the proceedings, the manslaughter convictions that the Adare gang had pleaded guilty to were condemned by delegate after delegate. 'Releasing prisoners is not a concession. They should never have been inside in the first place,' was the stated position of the Ógra Sinn Féin, youth wing of the party.

One of the endless assembly line interpretations and versions that Sinn Féin put into public circulation about the early release provisions of the British-Irish Agreement was floated at that Ard Fheis by the party Vice President, Pat Doherty. Claiming that all prisoners held in the north and south were entitled to early release, he maintained, 'Qualifying prisoners are those nominated by their own spokesperson, namely the officer commanding.'

Warning that the northern conflict could not be resolved unless all political prisoners were released, he said, 'The current position is that all remaining IRA prisoners have been nominated as qualifying. We now await, in fact we demand, the immediate release of all those still in jail.'

At every twist and turn in the complex peace process negotiations, the release of the Adare killers was at the centre of Sinn Féin demands in return for any concessions made by the IRA.

At the end of the trial, the Sinn Féin mouthpieces and media sources were predicting that the Adare killers would be out of prison by the year 2000. As 1999 approached an end, serious disquiet was stirred when it emerged that the prisoners in question were in line to be transferred to the open prison at Castlerea. That prompted suspicions that the prison regime under which they were being held was for some reason being relaxed. The fear was that the transfer to an open prison was to ease the way towards the early release continually being demanded in the peace process discussions.

In order to establish the government's thinking and position, a request for a meeting with the Minister for Justice was granted. The Minister met with Ann McCabe, her Garda son, John, and Ben O'Sullivan in November. The Minister not only allayed their worst fears; in the wake of that meeting he put the Government's position in writing.

In his letter of December 1999, the Minister wrote:

Dear Mrs McCabe,

I was glad to have the opportunity of meeting with yourself and your son John, Ben O'Sullivan and others on Wednesday last to hear at first hand your concern that the planned transfer of IRA prisoners from Portlaoise to Castlerea Prison might be a prelude, or be used as a pretext, for the early release from prison of those who were convicted in connection with the death of your late husband.

I hope that what I said at the meeting provided you with assurance that there is no question of granting early release to those concerned, either under the terms of the Good Friday Agreement or for that matter, on any other basis either. I want to reassure you now, formally and in writing, that the Government's position, right from the beginning, was that the men concerned are not covered by the terms of the Good Friday Agreement and that their transfer to Castlerea will have no bearing whatsoever on the question of early release. They will serve their time in Castlerea just as they would have in Portlaoise.

That said, I'm sure you will understand why, as the Minister with responsibility for prisons, I must, like all my predecessors, have discretion to decide where and how individual offenders will be held and managed within the prison system. It is a normal, and very regular part of day-to-day prison management to transfer prisoners from one prison to another – and prisoners convicted of the most serious offences are, and always have been, included in this process. My decision in the case of the group of prisoners who were convicted in connection with your husband's death is not, I can assure you, based on any thinking on my part that they should have some sort of preferential treatment. It is based on consultations and advice tendered to me from which it is clear that the transfer would be in the interests of better prisons management at this time. I cannot, no more than any of my predecessors could, outline all of the considerations which underlie decisions of this kind but, in order to assure you that there is nothing underhand involved, I can say that amongst the considerations presented to me is the need to free up and refurbish accommodation in Portlaoise. This refurbishment has now become essential and could not be achieved without the transfers to Castlerea.

I propose, therefore, to go ahead with the planned transfer of IRA prisoners from Portlaoise towards the end of next week, but, in so doing, I am absolutely assuring you that this has no early release implications whatsoever insofar as those convicted in connection with your husband's death are concerned.

John O'Donoghue TD
Minister for Justice, Equality and Law Reform

As the Adare killers went into the second year of their sentences, the heat was turned up from new quarters. The restored peace process was inching slowly along and, with each grudging concession from the paramilitaries, early release was being granted and killers of members of the security forces in Northern Ireland were returning to liberty. With media columnists and commentators scrambling for new aspects of the peace process to work over, no strenuous effort was needed to prompt them to pose questions as to why Ann McCabe should be spared the anguish and torment of seeing the men responsible for the death of her husband stroll through the streets of Limerick less than five years since they had shot him down.

On separate but familiar ground the well-oiled Sinn Féin machine continued its constant drip and ripple effect tactics on behalf of the Castlerea four, as they had come to be identified within the republican movement. With polished media skills that eclipsed the efforts of the major Dáil parties, and operating from the shadows in contrast to the hordes of high profile advisors left languishing in their wake, Sinn Féin made every chance count.

In what the media labels the 'silly season' when the absence of courts and other reliable providers of worthwhile news, and with the Dáil and Senate in recess, Sinn Féin hooked summer media coverage with the irresistible prospect of its supporting Fianna Fáil, the republican party, in the event of a Dáil deadlock following the next general election.

What emanated from Sinn Féin was that the release of the Adare killers would be part of the price to be extracted to support Fianna Fáil in a hung Dáil.

So what if a general election was almost two years away? And so what if the electorate and the analysts and others who weighed up political prospects would expect a great deal more than a demand for the release of imprisoned killers from a party with aspirations for some sort of role, however small, in government? This proposal allowed Sinn Féin increased media coverage and reassured the Castlerea prisoners that the pressure for their release was being maintained.

Minister for Justice, John O'Donoghue, reiterated the government's position which meant no change. For the media that meant that he was saying nothing new, but Sinn Féin was; by introducing the plausible, if remote, possibility of Fianna Fáil having to resort to support from Sinn Féin. Consequently, the media again turned to Ann McCabe. What did she think? What did she have to say?

The media were pressing a woman who was the daughter of a Garda and the widow of a slain Garda to deliver her thoughts on whether her husband's killers should be granted freedom so that Sinn Féin could prop up a Fianna Fáil government? What did they expect her to say? Again, what could she say? Besides the recycled and revisited agony involved, what possible difference or influence could her attitude have on the theoretical makeup of the next government?

Did the editorial plotters of the next day's headlines somehow contrive a scenario in which Ann McCabe would come out and say that if it was a matter of keeping Fianna Fáil in government or having to re-run a general election, she would reluctantly announce that, in the interests of political stability, she was prepared to see her husband's killers go free and she would release the Minister for Justice from his pledges given in writing? Like the Minister and Government, her position had been made clear. So why did they keep on asking?

However there was one voice that spoke up for Ann McCabe and her husband. That was the Association of Garda Sergeants and Inspectors. An article from its General Secretary, George Maybury, reflected the disquiet and continued concern in the middle management ranks of the Gardaí about possible Government wavering.

Responding to reports that legal proceedings were to be taken by the Adare killers to challenge their exclusion from the early release programme, the AGSI leader wrote:

> *The government must not step back one iota from its already strongly stated position that the killers of Detective Garda Jerry McCabe do not come within the ambit of the Good Friday Agreement, and therefore will not qualify for early release under its terms.*

'Additionally, there must be no equivocation on the part of the government,' Maybury stated when calling on the government to fight 'with all the legal resources at the command of the State'. He added that the great depth of feeling among Gardaí of all ranks could not be over-emphasised as well as 'their repugnance at the very fact that even a possible release under the agreement is the subject of public debate'.

> *The very fact that there is a debate, and how it is being fuelled by inspired leaks and weak statements, is causing great distress and anger to the Force which has served this State loyally and well through many turbulent years. The circumstances surrounding the killing of Garda McCabe, the serious wounding of Detective Garda Ben O'Sullivan and the subsequent court proceedings which were marked by wholesale intimidation of witnesses are well known and do not need repeating. Suffice to say that they fill all right-thinking persons with horror.*

Recalling the circumstances and initial disowning of the killers by the IRA and subsequent admission that IRA men were acting on their own initiative, the AGSI General Secretary went on to say:

> *In other words, the incident was an attempted robbery carried out by criminals during which a member of An Garda Síochána was shot dead and another seriously wounded. Under that definition, those convicted of the crimes clearly cannot come under the terms of the agreement reached between two sovereign governments and other parties.*

'The IRA cannot have it both ways,' George Maybury asserted. An unauthorised action could not be brought under the wing of the Good Friday Agreement 'by any stretch of credulity'.

While acknowledging that the strength of statements from Minister John O'Donoghue was heartening to Gardaí, the AGSI leader added a word of caution to the government:

> *A failure to come out strongly and say that any court action by the killers would be fought rigorously by the State will deepen a sense of unease which is also there in the Force. To say that Gardaí are beginning to feel betrayed already by less than forthright statements from other quarters would not be putting it too strongly.*

There could be no mistaking the pent up feelings within the Garda force and the overall message that was being sent out. It was spelled out in the final paragraph of the George Maybury article:

> *Gardaí all over this country will be watching and carefully weighing any statements and spins appearing in the media during these days. They will be watching for any lack of resolve on the part of government, either to live up to the promise that Jerry McCabe's killers will serve anything less than a significant sentence, or in its behaviour during any court action taken by the killers. Their morale and their sense of being valued by the State is at stake.*

Whatever the AGSI had to say, the ostensible Sinn Féin media strategy of constantly repeating the same message in the same phrases and soundbites irrespective of which of their spokespersons was involved, insinuated the Adare killers issue into every possible media opportunity. This time it was after a High Court hearing for the extradition of two wanted IRA men to Northern Ireland. This time it was Martin Ferris who, in November 2000, was consolidating his electoral base in Kerry as a member of both the Tralee and county local authorities that laid the ground for his 2002 capture of the North Kerry constituency seat of the former Labour Party leader, Dick Spring.

Already his party's nominee to contest the next general election, in the aftermath of the extradition hearing, he reached into the Sinn Féin bag of media tricks to reinvigorate the issue of the Adare killers and their incarceration. He did it on local radio with the certain intuition that whatever he had to say would be picked up by the print media.

The gist of what he had to say was that the government was prepared to 'give' on the sorting out of the extraditions situation but was not budging on the Adare issue.

On the air and in comments afterwards that got him the bonus of newspaper exposure the following day, the fisherman, turned IRA volunteer, turned full-time politician, took it upon himself to interpret the legalities of the Good Friday Agreement and how the government in the Republic was not honouring the terms of the agreement.

Once again stirring the pot of the coalition then in power, Councillor Ferris pinpointed 'political difficulties' as the reason why the government had 'not lived up fully' to the prisoner part of the agreement.

Confirming that he had been in touch with the Adare killers in Castlerea Prison, he said the four had been in discussions with their legal team that could lead to a court action challenging their detention.

The four were part of the IRA organisation, he asserted. They were IRA prisoners and they qualified for release. Councillor Ferris had no doubts about the authenticity of his legal analysis. 'Clearly they are within the Good Friday Agreement. There is nothing written into the agreement that bars their release,' he said, without any special emphasis on the 'written into' qualification. For good measure the former gun-runner and active service IRA Volunteer cautioned the government that the release of the Adare killers and all qualifying prisoners was 'imperative' and should take place soon.

The drip-drip tactics of Sinn Féin were working. They were being worked by remote control with Sinn Féin at arm's length and the media making the calls and asking the questions. The tactic of eroding away resistance was at work and was still a form of torture. But only for Ann McCabe. Pressure was being applied to the government through Ann McCabe, but nobody in government was speaking up for her.

As the paramilitary prisoners walked, the media and politicians in Northern Ireland latched onto what was perceived as the preferential treatment for Mrs McCabe in the government refusal to grant early release to the Adare killers. A new controversy was stirred up as the media searched out the widows and families of RUC, UDR and other members of the security forces in the North and canvassed their views on why the killers of Detective McCabe could remain locked up while the gunmen and bombers who operated in the killing fields across the border were being released.

It was to set out the facts and counter the fiction of the case that Ann McCabe consented to be interviewed for a BBC Northern Ireland *Spotlight* documentary which also included the widows of RUC men who had been killed in the northern conflict.

She went on in the knowledge that many who were close to her had very genuine reservations about the exercise and also amid most understandable anxiety from other quarters that she could be walking into a political trap, or at least into something which could seriously backfire.

She dreaded the entire experience, but nevertheless endured through what, for her, was the ordeal of a lengthy interview in her home on a Sunday afternoon. She had already learned to be most wary of the media, but she went in front of the lights and camera to set the record straight.

Her message was simple but had to be presented in a most sensitive way to avoid any offence or hurt to the widows and families of northern police officers who had suffered the same loss and anguish. The message was that the Adare case was different.

The Adare killing was different because, irrespective of whether a resumption of the armed struggle had been declared or not, the IRA was not at war with the security forces in the Republic. In fact, the Irish Republican Publicity Bureau front for the IRA and the IRA Army Council, plus its plants who fed the media appetite, were constantly proclaiming that Standing Order 8 expressly prohibited military action against the security forces of what Sinn Féin referred to as 'the South'.

On the other side of the border, the IRA and its propaganda machine not only maintained that members of the security forces of the North and Great Britain were 'legitimate targets', they also issued statements distorting the term 'responsibility' to new grisly meaning when claiming the kills for its gunmen and bombers.

Therefore the shootings in Adare that killed one detective and, only by sheer chance, spared a second, had not been directed against targets that were regarded either as the forces that the IRA was pitted against, or as legitimate targets. In fact, the opposite was the case under IRA military rules.

The Adare killing was different because in that case the IRA unit involved did not come under fire from Gardaí protecting a road shipment of cash. On the contrary, the detectives had been fired on while they sat unarmed in their car, their revolvers still in their belts and the Uzi sub machinegun locked away in its case behind them. If it was a wartime shooting, the gunning down of two policemen who did not have weapons to defend themselves would have been branded an atrocity and a war crime.

The Adare killing was different because those involved had been disowned by the IRA and their very involvement denied by Sinn Féin. When compelled to retract its denials and admit that members were involved, the IRA army council changed its tune to state that the operation had not been sanctioned and that the group involved had been acting independently. In other words, if it happened in a conventional war, the military personnel involved would be undertaking an unauthorised maverick action and operating outside the bounds of military regulation and therefore liable to court martial and punishment.

The difference in the conditions that the Adare killers were being held in also came under question and under public scrutiny in that same year. Why the IRA men were serving their sentences in a self-contained bungalow with access to a phone was the subject of a Dáil question from Des O'Malley. O'Malley, whose life had been under threat when he served as Minister for Justice at the start of the northern conflict, wanted to know why the jail conditions for the IRA men should be different from others convicted of non-paramilitary serious crime. He demanded to know if the phone bill for the Adare quartet was being met by the taxpayer or the IRA.

Deputy O'Malley was told that the conditions were nothing special. It was also explained from government sources that the bungalow had very basic fittings and the telephone was a card payphone. While the Minister for Justice had told Ann McCabe and Ben O'Sullivan five months earlier that the move to Castlerea of the IRA men had been to make room for refurbishment at Portlaoise Prison, a different explanation was given in March 2000. Then it was stated that the move was part of a government understanding with the republican movement which was central to the IRA ceasefire.

Nine months later it emerged that two of the IRA men had been given temporary releases from Castlerea and, while they were out, had been caught breaking the law in after-hours drinking. It also emerged that the prison authorities had slipped up in not notifying Ann McCabe of the temporary releases which posed the possibility of her encountering one or other of her husband's killers.

But Mrs McCabe was not the only one who had not been informed that the two were at liberty. Limerick member of the Garda Representative Association national executive, Paul Browne, hit out at the failure to inform local Gardaí that the pair could turn up in their vicinity. 'Certainly it would be the practice that the Gardaí would be told. This was a practice broken,' he said.

It was revealed that while on temporary leave on compassionate grounds to visit his sick mother, Jeremiah Sheehy had been among after-hours drinkers found during a Sunday night Garda check on compliance with the licensing laws at the Rathkeale Inn where Sheehy was in the company of a woman. Gardaí then also revealed that when Pearse McCauley had been granted temporary release in October 2000, he too was found drinking after hours in a pub in Lifford, county Donegal. He had also been set free on compassionate grounds to visit his sick father.

But while the two had been caught in late night drinking sessions, the Department of Justice stated that no reports of breaches of the conditions of the temporary releases had been received by the prison authorities. If breaches had been reported, they would have been fully investigated, the Department stated.

A denial that Sheehy had stayed in a hotel with a woman in his native Rathkeale was released by the Sinn Féin spokesman in west Limerick, Cyril MacCurtain. He said he had been contacted by the officer commanding the republican prisoners in Castlerea, Kevin Walsh, who had been named in the Adare case as the leader of the armed robbery attempt. Walsh had relayed a message that he had spoken with Sheehy who denied that he stayed at any hotel with a woman and had overnighted at the address that he provided on his temporary release form.

The GRA's Paul Browne said that he had no objection to prisoners socializing while on temporary release but added, '… the Gardaí should be informed and apprised of the fact that prisoners such as those convicted of very serious crimes are out.' He said that while it was his understanding that Gardaí in the relevant districts were informed if prisoners from their area were being given temporary release, this had not happened in the case of Jeremiah Sheehy. He said the local Garda who had encountered Sheehy in the pub had been stunned.

That there had been some breakdown in communication was indicated when the Minister of State at the Department of Justice, Mary Wallace, told the Dáil in the following week that the Minister, John O'Donoghue, had requested procedures to be put in place that would ensure that Ann McCabe was informed of future releases.

The very prompt manner in which Sinn Féin and the IRA moved to counter and deny the most damaging claims about the early releases can be attributed to a letter which was sent to *The Limerick Leader*.

The letter was from the Rev Michael Nuttall, who, as Archdeacon, was the holder of an office directly below the Bishop of the diocese and who had his residence in Adare. His forceful public letter posed questions for the Government, the prison authorities and for the hotel that Sheehy had allegedly stayed in.

The Archdeacon challenged the Minister for Justice to explain why two men convicted for their part in the Adare killing of four and a half years earlier had been released back into the community without any instructions or notification to Gardaí that they were back in temporary circulation.

'How does it happen that such men were allowed home unguarded when prisoners serving a sentence for far less serious crimes than manslaughter have to be accompanied by prison officers even for a visit to hospital?' the Archdeacon demanded.

He reflected much of the sentiments expressed by Deputy Des O'Malley when questioning the regime under which the killers were serving their sentences. Referring back to the morning in which the people of Adare had awoken to the shattering events of the post office shooting, the Archdeacon's letter continued, 'We need to know now why men who perpetrated these crimes – who have already been transferred to Castlerea, a prison with a more relaxed regime than their previous place of detention – now have even more privileges bestowed upon them.' Rev Nuttall described the early releases as 'yet one more insult' heaped on the McCabe family.

The local eruption over the circumstances and events of the early releases was added to in the lead up to Christmas 2000 when a new mural was unveiled on the Falls Road, heartland of republicanism in Belfast, depicting the 'Castlerea Five' (the four who pleaded guilty to manslaughter, and the fifth convicted for conspiracy) and wishing them a happy Christmas.

In that same week, Sinn Féin ended the year with another repetition of the demand for the early release of the Adare killers. This time it came from party chairman, Mitchel McLoughlin, and this latest rerun of the message was delivered through the media in Cork.

The Sinn Féin chairman was in Cork to visit the North Central constituency in the Glasheen, Evergreen and St Finbarr's Hospital area of the city. The purpose was to bolster the party's effort to take one of the five Dáil seats in the constituency. The chairman took a double political potshot when combining the Castlerea prisoner release campaign with a subliminal message in a Fianna Fáil stronghold that the Adare killers might well be free, only for the unyielding stance of the Progressive Democrats in the government partnership.

'The government is playing it tough because the PDs have threatened to walk out of the coalition if these men are released early,' the Sinn Féin chairman claimed in the constituency of his PD counterpart, John Minihan.

Asked why Sinn Féin had not challenged the refusal to grant early release to the IRA men, Mr McLoughlin said, 'Our preference is to resolve this matter through political engagement but we would not rule out legal action.'

The Sinn Féin party chairman was then seemingly unaware that solicitor Michael Farrell was already engaged in assembling documentation to bring a court action on behalf of two of the Adare IRA men, Michael O'Neill and John Quinn, challenging the refusal of the government to include them under the early release provisions of the Good Friday Agreement. It would be revealed in the following year that the solicitor was already in contact with the Department of Justice and seeking information under the Freedom of Information Act in September 2000. But Mitchel McLoughlin was stating that court action was not the preferred option when he spoke with the media three months later, in mid-December.

In the opening days of August 2001, summer brightness was again darkened for Ann McCabe and her family. Then, in the High Court, the prospect that the killers of her husband could find an alternative route out of Castlerea was opened up when two of the Adare gang were granted leave to challenge their detention. Michael O'Neill, serving 11 years, and John Quinn, serving six, were granted judicial review of their claim that they were eligible for release under the Good Friday Agreement. The court hearing brought the early release issue back into the headlines and the shadow would hover for a further 18 months of the possibility that the doors of Castlerea could be opened to the IRA men.

The Adare trial was back in the courts and the headlines two months later. This time it was the State bringing the action and appealing the leniency of the 14 year sentences imposed on Kevin Walsh and Pearse McCauley. That hearing before the three judges of the Court of Criminal Appeal, with the Chief Justice presiding, served to reignite the public debate over the manslaughter plea that the State prosecution had consented to in the Special Criminal Court.

Although turning down the appeal for longer sentences brought by the Director of Public Prosecutions, the appeal court judges stated that the Adare case was 'characterised by a callous disregard for human life'. On that account the judges indicated that they would not have 'interfered' if the sentences had been for 17 years. The Chief Justice, Mr Ronan Keane, pointed out that the sentences on Walsh and McCauley were among the longest imposed in modern times for the offence of manslaughter.

It was clear that a long custodial sentence was appropriate for a crime which the court regarded as being 'at the most serious end of the scale of manslaughter offences'. Had the sentences been even longer 'it might very well be' that the appeal court would not interfere when taking into account 'the record of the accused men and the serious nature of their offences,' the judgement said.

However, when taking into account the period of custody before the 1999 trial, time being served would be equal to a sentence of 15 years with remission. That, for the judges of the Court of Criminal Appeal, was a 'substantial departure from what would be appropriate'.

The goading and baiting of the McCabe family and the authorities continued in November when Kevin Walsh was granted temporary release from Castlerea to visit his sick father at his Patrickswell home. But Walsh turned up to address a meeting of republicans in Tipperary. While the storm of protest and criticism which followed other early releases had brought reassurances from departmental and prison authorities, they were again found lacking. Local Gardaí said that there had been no sign of Walsh in the Patrickswell area and Mrs McCabe had not been told.

Voicing her fears that the creeping concessions to the Adare killers would serve as the forerunner to early release, the Garda widow said, 'This man was released on so-called compassionate grounds. But where was the compassion for me and my family by allowing this man onto the streets of Limerick?'

At the end of that year, the Taoiseach was still resolute and reported to be resisting the continued Sinn Féin overtures in northern talks to bring the prison release into the overall package to be traded in return for IRA decommissioning.

The big jolt, and reminder of attitudes towards authority and rules that put the Adare killing back in the headlines, came in August 2003 when the killers were smiling and relaxed as they looked out from the pages of the national media. With them were four Sinn Féin Deputies elected to Dáil Eireann. The TDs were the party leader in the Dáil,

Caoimhghin Ó Caoláin, Sean Crowe, Aengus Ó Snodaigh and Martin Ferris. They were pictured with four republican prisoners, inside the precincts of Castlerea Prison where taking of photographs is prohibited.

The photograph was taken in the prison on 16 August and appeared in the Sinn Féin newspaper *An Phoblacht/Republic News*.

In the uproar and expressions of outrage that followed, Martin Ferris explained why all but Deputy Arthur Morgan of the party's complement of five members of the Dáil had visited Castlerea Prison as a group. The purpose, Deputy Ferris said, had been to update the republican prisoners on the peace process, and particularly on the status of the talks taking place at the time.

He said the photograph had appeared in the republican newspaper along with a report on the meeting. The paper, he said, 'is bought and read by republicans and that was the purpose of the photograph appearing there.' He added that he did not believe that the prison rules had been breached.

In that view Deputy Ferris could not have been more remote from the official attitude of the prison authorities. The Director General of the Prison Service, Sean Aylward, issued a statement which said that from initial inquiries, there had been a clear breach of prison rules. Adding that the taking of the picture was 'a cause for concern', the governor at the prison had been asked for a full report into the circumstances in which the breach took place.

Mr Aylward also ordered an immediate review of visiting arrangements at the prison to ensure full compliance with the governor's orders.

Once again the prison service had to offer apologies to the McCabe family. With the family shocked and distressed by the pictures, Mr Aylward's statement said, 'The prison service regrets any distress caused by the publication of this photograph.'

The McCabe family reaction to the picture was reflected by the 'shock and anger' registered by the chairman of the Progressive Democrats, John Minihan. Calling for an enquiry into the breach of prison rules, he commented, 'This latest stunt by Sinn Féin is an affront to democracy and is grossly insulting and distressing to the family of the late Jerry McCabe.'

It took five years, during which Sinn Féin and occasional allies waged a relentless campaign of opposition, for the stance of Justice Minister, John O'Donoghue, to be vindicated.

The position he had made clear from 1998 and spelled out in some detail in the special Dáil debate after the Adare trial, was affirmed in the High Court judgement of March 2003 on the application of two of the Adare case convicts for early release under the terms of the Good Friday Agreement.

In the course of his 40-page reserved judgement, Mr Justice Michael Peart reaffirmed what the Minister had stated and restated time after time: that early release was at the discretion of the Minister for Justice, whose nomination of prisoners for early release was essential. The case put for the two prisoners included submissions that they were being discriminated against because others who had committed similar crimes had been released. At the time more than 500 prisoners had been released, 444 in Northern Ireland and 57 in the Republic. But it was the ruling of the court that there was no obligation on the Minister to either consider the men's application or to specify that they qualified.

Mr Justice Peart's judgement acknowledged that the men were 'qualifying prisoners' under the terms of the Good Friday Agreement, but held that 'no individual rights were conferred on the men by the agreement'.

'In not sanctioning their release, the Minister for Justice was exercising an executive function of a discretionary nature,' the judgement stated. 'The courts could interfere only if those powers had been exercised in a capricious, arbitrary or unjust way.'

It was revealed in government documents released for the case that the decision to exclude the Adare killers from eligibility for early release was to 'protect' support for the Good Friday Agreement.

The document, released under the Freedom of Information Act to the defence team for one of the men, stated that it 'was not a case of applying different standards in the case of persons convicted of the murder of Gardaí. Persons convicted of the murder of other Gardaí, who have already served long sentences, will be covered by the prisoner release arrangements.'

Yet even with the High Court ruling that the State had been within its rights and had not acted incorrectly, the Sinn Féin offensive was maintained by Deputy Martin Ferris. 'I am conscious of the pain and upset of the McCabe family, but the Castlerea prisoners qualify under the terms of the Good Friday Agreement and there is an obligation on the government to honour their commitments and release them,' he insisted after the High Court decision had been handed down.

Deputy Ferris was back making public statements about the killers of Detective McCabe when he was priming the political pump for the 2004 Sinn Féin Ard Fheis in an important election year.

In the lead up to the party assembly, he said in a radio interview, 'The IRA have said in the recent past that they apologise for all non combatants who died in this campaign. They have also said in the past that there was no intention to kill Garda McCabe, so I accept that.'

'Over the last 30 years a lot of things happened that should not have, and a lot of suffering has been inflicted on people, including the McCabe family. We have made our position quite clear on this. That it should not have happened, but it happened,' he said.

The north Kerry TD went out further than ever on a legal limb when claiming that Garda evidence had been presented at the Adare trial to bear out his contention. 'The Special Criminal Court accepted evidence from senior Garda officers that this was not premeditated or not deliberate,' he claimed.

The theme was taken up again in the keynote speech to his party Ard Fheis by the Sinn Féin President, Gerry Adams.

Reflecting the low ebb in relations with the Government at the time, he said that both the Irish and British governments had to face up to the reality that republicans had very little confidence in them and their commitment to the Good Friday Agreement.

As a co-guarantor of the agreement, the Irish government was failing to deliver on issues, Mr Adams charged, and said the issues included 'prisoners within this jurisdiction who should have been released'.

At a time of what he termed a 'dangerous crisis', he said the great challenges were to get the British government to embrace a strategy to bring an end to the union and to work to bring about a united and independent Ireland.

'But why should a British government move on these democratic objectives or even on the Good Friday Agreement when others will accept less?' he asked. Saying that efforts to put Sinn Féin under pressure were 'a waste of time' and that the party would not be bullied, Mr Adams directed his charges and challenges at the Taoiseach, Bertie Ahern. 'Nationalists and republicans,' he said, 'looked to the Irish government to persuade the British government on these matters.'

In the run up to May local and European Parliament elections, which would be a test of strength and support for all parties, Sinn Féin stepped up the pressure on the Irish government, in particular, to deliver. A great deal was to unfold over the remainder of 2004.

Chapter 19

With stunning shock effect, everything was changing. All bets were off and the solemn commitments, written assurances and sincere promises were a thing of yesterday.

The shock was double-edged.

This time the government was rowing back.

Worse still, the government had been relenting and conceding ground since the previous year and the Adare killers could have been free in October 2003. Only the Ulster Unionists and, in part, the obstinacy of the IRA not to be seen to concede full demands, had kept the four in Castlerea.

That the government had been trading what they had pledged never to concede, began to seep out in May 2004.

Even so, there had been some hints in the previous year that something was afoot which could involve a u-turn by government. In response to a Dáil question from Labour leader Pat Rabbitte, Bertie Ahern had confirmed that 'the Jerry McCabe issue is outstanding and we are considering it'. That statement was made to the Dáil towards the end of 2003, but it was to emerge that the release of the Adare killers had been on the negotiating table as far back as March of that year and that, if agreement had been reached then, the four would have been set for early release in October 2003.

It transpired that the parties involved in the northern talks to end conflict and establish a power-sharing administration had been within an ace of getting agreement from all sides for the entire package. With Sinn Féin adamantly holding out for the release of the Adare killers, the negotiators for Bertie Ahern's government were conceding that consent to their freedom would be part of a settlement once it was clear that IRA criminality, as well as its paramilitary activities, would cease permanently.

Not for months did it emerge that the deal collapsed when Ulster Unionist Leader, David Trimble, pulled the plug. He scuppered the deal at the last minute because his party was not satisfied with the act of decommissioning of IRA weapons that had been demanded. Although an act of putting weapons out of commission did take place, the IRA continued to hold back on any gesture or action that could possibly be interpreted or proclaimed by its opponents, political and otherwise, as surrender. Therefore, the IRA refused permission to the head of the International Decommissioning Body, General John de Chastelain, to disclose the full details of the decommissioning act. Because that failed to meet what was called for, the Ulster Unionists said no.

David Trimble's Ulster Unionists had held their line. It appeared that the Government in the Republic had not, and that came as a shock even to the Democratic Unionist Party of Rev Ian Paisley.

When what had almost happened the previous October came into the open, the DUP deputy leader, Peter Robinson, commented that he was 'deeply disturbed' that the Garda McCabe killers could have been released.

It also emerged that David Trimble had been in the dark about the willingness of the Government in the Republic to go back on its guarantees. Mr Trimble said in May 2004 that he had known nothing of that aspect of the plan, but contended that it justified his decision not to accept what had been on offer the previous October.

Confirmation that the release of the Adare IRA gunmen was now a part of the northern peace and decommissioning package came from the Taoiseach at the launch of his Fianna Fáil party's 2004 local election big push in Dublin. The shock waves that radiated out from the admission became a storm by the time the Dáil resumed the following week.

Accused in the Dáil of a 'secret, dirty deal with the IRA' by the Fine Gael leader, Enda Kenny, the Government was not only changing its stance but changing the ground.

To sidestep the written assurances given to Ann McCabe, the government line now was that the release of the Adare killers was under consideration, not under the Good Friday Agreement, but under the provisions of the new deal which had been hammered out the previous October and which included measures and actions that had not been covered by the Good Friday document. Distinctions were also being made in government utterances. The Department of Justice issued a statement which suggested that release as part of a deal was possible. But the Department of Justice statement also sidestepped the pledges that had been made by the former incumbent of the justice office, John O'Donoghue. While John O'Donoghue had spelled it out in the Dáil that any release of the Adare prisoners required a nomination from him as Minister, and that it was not going to happen, a qualification was now added in. The Department of Justice statement said that the government had always made it clear that it would not authorise any such release in the context of continued paramilitarism.

The onus for authorising release was being switched from the Minister for Justice to the government, even though the statement was coming from the Department of Justice.

The statement from the Department of Justice was also making a distinction that the early releases demanded by Sinn Féin would only get government consideration if the IRA ceased all its activities.

But the letter from Minister O'Donoghue to Ann McCabe in November 1999 did not confine itself to the possibility of early release under the terms of the Good Friday Agreement. The Minister's letter was categoric that, 'there is no question of granting early release to those concerned, either under the terms of the Good Friday Agreement or for that matter, on any other basis either.'

Now hounded by the opposition, the Taoiseach was asking the Dáil to look at things from a different point of view. He said it was 'unhelpful' to be taking any single element of an agreement 'and try to deal with it outside the only context in which it has relevance'. The issues and matters that had been under negotiation the previous year included the question of on-the-run prisoners, and the Castlerea prisoners were, the Taoiseach said, 'not unrelated' but, he added, 'neither are they covered by the Good Friday Agreement.'

The Taoiseach was defending the concessions that his negotiators had been prepared to trade, but stressing that the concessions would only be made if the IRA also delivered. The 'goal' he said was to clear all outstanding issues 'including the republican movement finally, and definitely, making a historic move away from violence'.

The Taoiseach took pains to go over the ground in detail again and again in the Dáil exchanges. 'Let me be clear. For its part, the government can consider the early release of these prisoners only in the context where the achievement of all other acts of completion, as set out, are assured.'

The Labour leader, Pat Rabbitte, declared that it was 'unacceptable to introduce the release of the McCabe killers as pawns in negotiations'. This brought another reiteration of the government's stance from the Taoiseach but gave Mr Ahern the opportunity of reworking the case in easier to comprehend terms. It had to be made '100 per cent clear' the Taoiseach said, 'that consideration by the government of releasing the Castlerea five would only be in terms of the end of paramilitarism and a final agreement.'

The Fine Gael leader, Deputy Enda Kenny, saw things in a different light. 'The Provisional IRA now believes it will get whatever it demands in return for the fulfillment of its commitment,' he told the Taoiseach.

Saying that there was an enormous range of issues involved, the Taoiseach put the government view in starker terms. 'If we ever want to get an end to the IRA, which is what I want, we will have to be brave and take some pain to get some gain.'

The Taoiseach said he was aware of the difficulties involved in releasing the prisoners. 'We would have to engage in discussions with the families which we would do, and with the Garda representative bodies,' he told the Dáil.

For the government, the disclosures and admissions to what had almost happened the previous year came at the wrong time. Elections to the European Parliament from the entire island and to local councils in all twenty-six counties of the Republic were less than six weeks away and, on all counts, Sinn Féin was making an all out effort to top up the electoral gains the party had already made in the North and the Republic.

This time Sinn Féin was holding its collective tongue on the release of the Adare killers but not because the party's relentless campaign might lose votes. Going into the June 2004 elections, the government was now making the case for the release of the IRA gunmen from Castlerea.

But public opinion was emphatically against that course. Having published the full text of the formal letter from the Minister for Justice to Ann McCabe in 2000, *The Irish Examiner* followed up the next week with an opinion poll that showed almost three quarters of those surveyed in the newly-shaped south constituency for the European Parliament election were opposed to granting of early release. Even more compelling was the finding from the survey that 73 per cent of those questioned were against the concession of early release, even in the event of a halt to all IRA activities.

The opinion poll was jointly commissioned by the Cork-based national daily newspaper and the *Prime Time* current affairs programme on RTÉ. On that programme, Ann McCabe once again had to make the point that she and her family had to find out about the possible release of her husband's killers through IRA/Sinn Féin. It had been left to her and her family to make contact with the government for guidance on how its new position could be reconciled with the written guarantee in her possession.

The timing was all wrong, and wrong on the double, for the former Minister for Justice, Gerry Collins. Bidding to hold his seat in the European Parliament in the Munster constituency which had been shorn of one of its seats, he was already under pressure from his own running mate and fellow MEP, Brian Crowley. His stronghold was in the Limerick area where his family had held political sway for Fianna Fáil since the foundation of the party. His Abbeyfeale home was on the border of county Limerick, where the Adare atrocity had taken place, and adjoining the native Kerry county of Jerry McCabe. It was his ill luck that on the day that, what Fine Gael Enda Kenny has termed the 'dirty deal' details were being flushed out in the Dáil, Gerry Collins was on the election trail in Kerry. It was no surprise that he was questioned on Radio Kerry about the turnabout in the government's attitude to the early release for the Adare gunmen, and no surprise either that the MEP stated that he would 'not at all' favour early release. One of the elders of the Fianna Fáil party who had held high office in the party structure, as well as in cabinet, since the late 1960s, he promised that he would be conveying his views to the Taoiseach 'in as strong a way as I can to those in government'.

Closer to home, back in the Limerick city core of the Limerick East constituency, the political flak was also flying. Rocked by the news that all was set for the release of the Adare killers the previous October, Ann McCabe issued a statement which said that the only consolation for her and the McCabe family through the years of torment since the loss of her husband had been 'the trust in the integrity of the pledges formally given by government that the rulings of the recognised lawful courts of the land would be complied with.'

The statement said:

> *As the undertakings given by government were sealed with the lifeblood of a guardian of the law cruelly slain in the performance of his duties on behalf of the civil power, the position of the McCabe family is unchanged. Because of its trust that the stance of government is also unchanged, the McCabe family sees no need for additional comment.*

Unchanging too was the attitude of Minister of State, Tim O'Malley, who had succeeded to the Limerick East seat of his cousin, Des O'Malley, in 2002. He had discussions with the party leader and Tánaiste, Mary Harney, and with the party president and Minister for Justice, Michael McDowell, before issuing a 'no way' statement.

'There will be no change in attitudes whatsoever,' he said. 'No way do these people conform to any Good Friday Agreement. We will make that clear to everyone including Fianna Fáil.' But Deputy O'Malley, who had been raised to the rank of Minister of State on his entry to the Dáil, did qualify his declaration of total opposition. 'There is no way these killers should be left out of prison until all paramilitary activities have ceased. That includes both loyalists and the provisionals. We are nowhere near that situation. The will of the people of Ireland must be met first before the issue can even be considered,' he said.

****

The top vote getter and senior political figure in Limerick East, Willie O'Dea, had finally achieved his ambition of cabinet rank when he was nominated as Minister for Defence in the 2004 administration led by the Fianna Fáil party he had represented in the Dáil since February 1982.

Never short of political darts for his opponents, and exceptionally sure footed in political balancing acts, he had been the butt of celebrated mockery in the Dáil from his longtime local adversary, Jim Kemmy. The Limerick socialist, who died in 1998, had ridiculed Deputy O'Dea as 'meek as a mouse in the Dáil, but Mighty Mouse back in Limerick'.

While others were unchanged in their views, Minister O'Dea at least changed his mind and his public statements over a period of a week. In the immediate local uproar that the revelations about the early release near-miss caused, Minister O'Dea was unequivocal. His statement to the local media that the killers should not be released, and should not be considered for release, prompted media interpretations that he was squaring up to defy the government in which he was a serving cabinet Minister.

Minister O'Dea also had his own interpretation of what the negotiations of the previous October had involved. 'When things were discussed at that time, all kinds of things were being discussed, and maybe that was floated and from what side, I am not sure,' he told *The Limerick Leader.*

He said he would be 'shocked and horrified if such an offer had been made. It should not have been made and should not even be suggested or even mooted. But it should not happen either. I want to send out that clear signal now. It is out of bounds.'

The signal did change however. Back in Dublin the following week he told *The Irish Times* that he would accept 'with regret' the release of the killers 'if that was the only thing blocking a final settlement'.

While acknowledging that he had opposed the release in all circumstances, he said he had never envisaged a situation 'where it would be the only thing standing between final settlement and no settlement'.

'Whatever about my personal feelings, it's a matter for the government and the government's top priority is to solve this,' he said.

In the case of Sinn Féin, it was not just a case of no change on their part, but the party actually attempted to spread the responsibility for the fatal Adare shooting to the other parties involved in the northern peace process.

The Sinn Féin chairman, Mitchel McLaughlin, ventured into the raging cauldron of Limerick in the middle of May to marshal support for Sinn Féin candidates running in the June 2004 local elections and the European election in Munster.

Reflecting feelings in the city, the local media was not in the mood for soft interviews and pressed the Sinn Féin chairman. He said that it was impossible for him to conceive that some prisoners would remain in prison if there was to be closure or finalisation of the peace process. Cautioning that the release of the Adare killers did not have to be an electoral issue, he added, 'If people are seriously concerned about Ann McCabe, then they would be very careful about how they use this issue and whether they exploit this issue. Because this issue is going to be resolved. It is going to be painful. Does it have to be more painful for Ann McCabe than it is already?'

He described the Adare killing as 'this tragic incident' and was asked if Sinn Féin would make an apology to the McCabe family.

'It is my genuine response that it is a matter of intense regret,' Mr McLaughlin said. 'Do we apologise; do we accept responsibility for what happened to Garda McCabe? If people are prepared to recognise that we were all part of a moment of failure that resulted in the collapse of the IRA cessation during which period the Garda McCabe killing occurred, they should also share that responsibility. So would you be asking anyone else to apologise?'

Whether the killing of Detective McCabe and the campaign for the release of his killers was an election issue in Limerick, is known only to the voters. But while Sinn Féin made significant gains in representation and support in the elections to the European Parliament and the local authorities of the Republic, the pattern was not duplicated in Limerick city or county.

In the election for Limerick County Council, Sinn Féin support came to a maximum of 3.6 per cent in the two electoral areas of Kilmallock and Newcastle West where the party fielded candidates. In the election for Limerick City Council, there was a marked contrast in support for the two Sinn Féin candidates. In the four-seat Ward Two, Nancy Irwin secured 240 first preference votes which converted to a 4.6 per cent share of that vote. The exception occurred in Ward One, where a first preference poll of 568 votes brought the Sinn Féin candidate into the final shake up for the fifth seat. He was Maurice

Quinlivan from Ballynanty, brother of Nessan Quinlivan, IRA volunteer, who was captured, imprisoned and escaped from Brixton Prison in England with Pearse McCauley of the Adare killers active service unit.

In the Munster constituency race for election to the European Parliament, Fianna Fáil surrendered a seat held by longtime cabinet incumbent and party heavyweight, Gerry Collins. Six weeks before polling day he had publicly and explicitly distanced himself from the revised government stance on the release of the Adare IRA gang. While there were many influencing factors, including the reduction of Munster seats from four to three, the two seats held by Fianna Fáil from the first Euro elections of 1979 were reduced to one. The loss was to the comparative newcomer to politics and independent candidate with no party or established support structures to fall back on, the campaigner Kathy Sinnott.

The Fianna Fáil party of Bertie Ahern took a beating in the local elections while Sinn Féin made gains in virtually every contest, with conspicuous exceptions such as in Limerick and adjoining Clare. In the elections to the European Parliament, Fianna Fáil was the big loser with two seats less filled. Fianna Fáil representation in Brussels and Strasbourg was reduced from six to four while Sinn Féin won a seat in Dublin, went dangerously close in the North West, and turned in respectable performances in Munster and Leinster constituencies.

The reverses for the Taoiseach and his party in public opinion and electoral support were eased somewhat by Sinn Féin and the IRA. At the end of July, the IRA officially announced an end of warfare and a finish to the armed struggle and physical force. As a public demonstration that guerilla war was being abandoned, the IRA abandoned its traditional mode of communication under the pseudonym 'P O'Neill' and put a face and name on the official announcement. Ex-prisoner Seanna Walsh went before the cameras to make the announcement.

Two months later it was announced that the IRA had put its weapons out of commission. But the Democratic Unionist Party of the Rev Ian Paisley had its doubts. While the destruction of IRA weapons had been witnessed by two churchmen, the DUP required visual proof. They wanted photographs. The DUP contended that pictorial proof was not too much to ask. Sinn Féin's leaders said they would ask the IRA leadership.

As 2004 and further months of intricate cross-communication and concession trading in the northern peace process entered its final months and weeks, everything was on for Sinn Féin.

The return of a power-sharing assembly and administration for the North was on. Decommissioning destruction of IRA arms in a manner that would satisfy unionist demands for transparency and photographic proof were on, and that meant that the release of the Adare killers was also on.

What was happening was 'not on' for Des O'Malley who had retired from the Dáil at the 2004 election, having represented Limerick East since 1968. 'Not on' also for the former Minister for Justice was the spying operation on himself and other members of the Oireachtas for which a Sinn Féin election worker for Dublin Dáil Deputy, Aengus Ó Snodaigh, had been convicted in court. The longtime intermediary for successive Fianna Fáil administrations in liaison with the nationalist and republican communities in the North in particular, Senator Martin Mansergh, reflected the disquiet about criminality and a perception that the laws of the land did not apply in their case, when he described the 'aggressive and unapologetic' attitude of Deputy Ó Snodaigh as 'the unacceptable face of southern Sinn Féin'.

Strains and divisions were showing up in government which allowed an opportunity for the opposition.

On 1 December, Fine Gael leader Enda Kenny tabled a Dáil motion which led to confirmation from Taoiseach Bertie Ahern that the killers of Detective Jerry McCabe would be released once the DUP demands were satisfied by the IRA and Sinn Féin.

On the following day, as the media picked up on the resurrection of the early release concession, Ann McCabe made a one line statement to the television news. 'Who is running our government – Sinn Féin, the IRA or Bertie Ahern?' she asked. Like most unravellings, it started with one line.

Under fire and under stress, the coalition parties still clung to demonstrations of solidarity. Two days later, Tánaiste Mary Harney, successor as PD leader to Des O'Malley and his most trusted political ally, came out in support of the Taoiseach's line, adopting the view that however unpalatable it might be, getting a once and for all end to the IRA and its activities would require the government to swallow the words of honour it had given since November 1999.

Even Minister for Justice Michael McDowell was wavering. The former Attorney General and President of the Progressive Democrats was the arch critic of IRA/Sinn Féin which he consistently identified as one and the same, and lost no opportunity of attacking its criminality and lawlessness outside of its armed struggle. He too was edging up to toe the government line. On 6 December, he went on the prime radio news bulletin of the day to say that it would be the happiest day of his life if he had to travel to Limerick to tell Ann McCabe and her family that the killers who robbed them of a husband and father were to be released as the price of peace.

The price was too high for Des O'Malley. He emerged from the political shadows with the ghost of Jerry McCabe, his Limerick security shadow over decades of government, on the front page of *The Sunday Independent*.

He accused the 'political, administrative and media establishments' of appeasing terrorism and intimidating Ann McCabe. The Garda widow had been unfairly represented by the establishments as an obstacle to the progressing of the peace talks, he charged.

'A woman who is entitled to our sympathy and support is instead depicted as standing in the way of progress.'

Inside, *The Sunday Independent* carried a dozen articles attacking Sinn Féin, including a rundown on the sequence of government commitments, guarantees and pledges in the 1999-2004 period under the heading *Broken Promises and the Betrayal of Ann McCabe*.

Accompanying the Des O'Malley broadside against the government where the party he had founded was a junior but influential partner, was a harrowing picture of her shot to death husband, which Ann McCabe had given the newspaper permission to publish. She echoed the sentiments of Des O'Malley when saying, 'It is unjust of Sinn Féin and the IRA to hold me hostage and make out I'm standing in the way of the peace process.' She added, 'We all signed up for peace,' in reference to the referenda conducted in the Republic and Northern Ireland to clear the way for peace negotiation concessions.

Two days later, the northern peace process was back on the rocks. When Sinn Féin relayed the IRA's rejection of the DUP demand for a photographic record of decommissioning, the prospective First Minister, Rev Ian Paisley, abandoned the talks for formation of a powersharing executive.

In the Republic, the Government tried to stick with its end of the bargains that had been made. But the cracks were already widening. Inside a week, the divisions inside the Progressive Democrats were clear to be seen. With Des O'Malley's daughter, Fiona, hovering on the backbenches, and party chairman, John Minihan, not hiding his unease, the latest O'Malley elected for Limerick East went public.

Tim O'Malley asserted that the Adare killers should serve their full terms in jail. In declaring a position which differed from that of the government, he said, 'My view is I represent east Limerick. People in east Limerick are unhappy about the whole thing. A lot of people, not alone in Limerick but around the country, have contacted me in the past week or two on this.'

He was not distancing himself completely from his party leader and Tánaiste, Mary Harney. He pointed out that she had said that in the event of complete verification of decommissioning, and an IRA statement that they would desist from all criminal activity, releases could then be considered. He then added, 'Anything can be considered in the future, but we are not near it now and I would prefer if it would not be considered at all. Before, when someone murdered a Garda, it was a life sentence. Are the people who murdered Jerry McCabe going to get early release? This is a very serious issue for a sovereign government.'

From Limerick East too, the senior Fianna Fáil man, Minister for Defence Willie O'Dea, had met with Ann McCabe and was carrying her deep distress and the grave disquiet of her family and the Garda Representative Association to the ears of the Taoiseach and cabinet. The junior Fianna Fáil deputy Peter Power was also publicly indicating that he could be compelled to withdraw his Dáil support by resigning the Fianna Fáil party whip.

What had become a political powder keg for the government in the Republic was defused – by the £35million hostage taking and robbery at the Northern Bank in Belfast a week before Christmas.

With the IRA immediately fingered for the biggest robbery ever staged in Ireland, the Taoiseach was fuming and made no attempt to hide it when he raged in public about the secret plotting that had been going on behind the smokescreen of the peace process negotiations, and its attendant demands from the IRA and Sinn Féin in return for an end to criminality as well as conflict.

Sinn Féin denied IRA involvement and stated that there was no proof. As the stains spread wider in follow-up raids and arrests in the Republic in connection with laundering of the Northern Bank robbery haul, Sinn Féin continued to maintain that nothing was proven against the IRA.

There was no doubting the fury within government over being duped and coming within a whisker of giving in to IRA and Sinn Féin demands. Although Sinn Féin continued to protest IRA innocence, within three weeks clear signals were coming from the government that the release of the Adare gunmen was now out of the question and off the agenda. That was confirmed officially by Bertie Ahern in February 2005.

That the early release campaign was now history for Sinn Féin was also made clear when the four IRA men issued a statement from Castlerea Prison. They apologised for the killing of Detective Garda Jerry McCabe and also said that they would not be pressing for early release so that they could not be used as 'political pawns or hostages' in the peace process.

The government said that, with the exception of the welcome apology to the McCabe family, the statement was 'irrelevant' because the Taoiseach had already made it clear that early release was off the negotiating table. Justice Minister Michael McDowell commented that the 'belated' statement simply recognised the reality that early release had been ruled out. Nevertheless, Martin Ferris said the party would continue to press for release, although it would not be part of the peace process negotiations.

The prisoners knitted into their statement that they were involved in 'an IRA operation in Adare in June 1996' when offering deep regret and apologies for the killing and the hurt and grief caused to the families. 'There was never any intent to attack any members of the Garda Síochána,' the statement said.

The latter denial of deliberate intent was greeted with outrage by the Garda Representative Association. 'The evidence of the attack clearly indicates that their actions on the day made no attempt to spare the lives of the Garda officers, firing into the vehicle not once, but twice, and after doing so they made no attempt to take the money, but left the scene.'

In Northern Ireland, the nationalist SDLP party described the statement as 'beyond belief' and unionists dismissed the statement as dishonest and selfish.

It was Pat Kearney, fellow Kerryman and onetime Garda colleague of his brother-in-law and friend, Jerry McCabe, who spoke for the McCabe family. Three months short of nine years since the Adare killing, and six years after the trial, his initial reaction was to describe the statement from the killers as 'self-serving hypocrisy'. But he elaborated, '... an apology is very late in the day and does not alleviate the loss. However, we are Christian people and an apology is always welcome from wrongdoers.'

Michael O'Neill is due for release in May 2007. Jeremiah Sheehy's term is due to finish in February 2008. Kevin Walsh and Pearse McCauley are to walk free from Castlerea Prison in August 2009.

Appendix 1

The mocking conduct and demeanour of the four IRA men facing charges of capital murder during and after the trial at the Special Criminal Court was noted by journalists covering the case and recorded by specialist writers.

Following publication in *The Irish Independent* of a descriptive report on the opening day of the hearing, the barristers appearing in defence of the four protested to the judges. The presiding judge, Mr Justice Richard Johnson, responded that the protests were noted.

The full texts of the articles from national daily newspapers are reproduced here by permission of the editors of *The Irish Independent* and *The Irish Examiner*.

Smirking Quartet Put On a Loathsome Show
by Miriam Lord

It must have been galling for the Gardaí to endure yesterday's courtroom performance by the four men charged with murdering one of their own.

Jeremiah Sheehy, Michael O'Neill and Kevin Walsh appeared totally unconcerned with the fact that they were facing the most serious criminal charges that can be brought against any individual in the State. They chatted, shared the occasional joke and behaved like people who had no real interest in the proceedings.

But it was Pearse McCauley's stomach-churning display of smirking bravado that was particularly hard to take. He radiated a sort of loathsome smugness.

Many officers in the Special Criminal Court looked into the unrelenting cheerfulness of his face, only to turn away with bitterness in their eyes. It wasn't difficult to see why.

Not because of what Pearse McCauley and his co-accused have or haven't done but more because their seemingly nonchalant attitudes screamed of disrespect.

The subject matter of this trial is very painful for a lot of people but that didn't stop Pearse McCauley from smiling his way through the opening day. Jeremiah Sheehy attempted to strike a similar sort of pose, but he couldn't sustain the same level of disdainful ennui.

Five men faced charges yesterday. Four of them sat together: the quartet who are charged with the callous murder of Detective Garda Jerry McCabe and the attempted murder of his colleague, Ben O'Sullivan. The fifth defendant, John Quinn, who faces a conspiracy charge, sat apart.

The similarities between the four are very striking. They wore dark suits, collars and ties and each sported a green ribbon on his right-hand lapel.

One after the other they rose and looked straight ahead, hands behind their backs like soldiers standing at ease, each man answering the charges with a loud and clear 'Not Guilty'.

First to reply was Michael O'Neill, a gaunt and dark-haired Limerick man who looks older than his 46 years. As O'Neill got to his feet, Pearse McCauley, who was sitting directly behind him, bit his lip as he smiled, like he was trying to stop himself from laughing out loud.

Next up was Jeremiah Sheehy (36), a big, craggy-faced man with an alarming crewcut, Desperate Dan jaw and heavy overhanging brows. He stood up and stifled a snigger before any question was put to him. He uttered his first 'Not Guilty' with a big smile.

Smug contentment

Again in the row behind, Pearse McCauley seemed to find something very funny. Nor could Sheehy resist yet another smirk.

Sheehy folded his bulk back onto the seat with a satisfied looking smile on his face. 'Gerard Pearse McCauley'. The man who once escaped from Brixton prison slowly got to his feet, flashing a breezy grin as he smoothed down his dark grey silk tie against his light grey, button-down shirt.

A pale-faced man with receding light-brown hair, he looked the picture of smug contentment.

It was Sheehy's and Walsh's turn to talk to each other this time, one leaning back and the other forward while McCauley calmly called out his answers. When Walsh's turn came – he is a dapper 42 year old with short fair hair and a neatly trimmed beard – he behaved just the same as the others.

But of the four, it was Pearse McCauley who stood out.

When the court rose and the four accused were ushered, smiling, from the dock, Pearse McCauley's voice rang around the courtroom.

'Hey, fancy seein' you here!' he said to a friend in the public gallery, like she had turned up at his party, a welcome but unexpected guest.

The case continues today.

The Irish Independent, 12 January 1999

Garda Paid a High Price for Peace Effort
by Brian Carroll
Security Correspondent

It was little wonder that Pearse McCauley could smirk as he was led away to begin a 14-year sentence for the manslaughter of Detective Garda Jerry McCabe.

On his lapel, he wore the green ribbon. Cynically fashioned on the white ribbon of peace which symbolises the desires of ordinary decent Irish men and women, the green ribbon stands for something altogether different.

Martin McGuinness wears it. Gerry Adams wears it. Martin Ferris wears it. The green ribbon symbolises support for the republican struggle and the release of all republican prisoners, or prisoners of war, as they call themselves.

Pearse McCauley knows all about political prisoner status. We have all seen him on television punching the air as he walks free from the court or from prison, as he did in November 1995, two years into a seven-year sentence.

The government of the day opened the prison doors for McCauley, over-riding the sentence of the courts, because the IRA was on ceasefire and political prisoners had to be released.

McCauley was released in time to witness the first IRA ceasefire turn to dust at Canary Wharf and in plenty of time to kill Detective Garda Jerry McCabe in June 1996.

Detective Garda McCabe said goodbye to his wife early on the morning of 7 June 1996. He was 52-years old, a husband, a father of five, a son and a brother. Within hours he was shot dead in Adare, the 'I support PEACE' sticker on his car adding an indelible pathos to a morning already marked by tragedy.

Yesterday, his widow Ann, sat with her usual dignity, wearing the white ribbon of peace, ignoring the smiles of her husband's killer.

Although the McCabe family have consciously chosen not to speak out about the plea bargaining in the case or the sentences, others have taken to the airwaves in their droves to express anger.

Sinn Féin are alone in saying Jerry McCabe's killers should be released by April 2000 under the Good Friday Agreement. Ironically that's when Pearse McCauley should have been released for his 1993 firearms offence. Instead he was allowed out early to kill.

No wonder then McCauley was smirking at the prospect of 14 years. Last week he was looking at 40 years without remission. This week it's 14 years. Next week, if Martin McGuinness, Martin Ferris and Gerry Adams and the green ribbon brigade get their way, who knows?

When McCauley walked free in November 1995 Jerry McCabe didn't know the price he and his family would pay for peace. We still don't.

The Irish Examiner, 6 February 1999

Appendix 2

Detective Garda Jerry McCabe was the thirteenth member of the Garda force to die in the course of duty since the first Garda killing by subversives following the outbreak of the Northern Ireland troubles in 1970. The same number of Gardaí had been killed in the period from the 1922 establishment of the force up to 1942, a year in which three Gardaí were shot dead but also marked the start of a sequence of 28 years free of Garda deaths while enforcing the law.

To record all those who gave their lives in addition to Detective McCabe, the full list is provided here, courtesy of the Garda Museum.

Garda Roll of Honour

1922 November 14 – **Garda Henry Phelan** (23) from county Laois, shot dead in Mullinahone, county Tipperary, when buying hurleys for a team that Gardaí had formed after station opened in Callan, county Kilkenny.
1923 December 3 – **Sgt James Woods** (23) from county Clare, shot dead during armed raid on Garda station in Scartaglen, county Kerry.
1924 January 29 – **Garda Patrick Joseph O'Halloran** (27) from Baltinglass, county Wicklow, died of wounds a day after he was shot attempting to arrest two armed raiders.
1924 May 7 – **Sgt Thomas Griffin** (25) from Cork city, shot attempting to arrest armed criminal at Cregg, Carrick-on-Suir and **Garda John Alphonsus Murrin** (26) from Donegal, died of wounds from same shooting in September of that year.
1925 December 12 – **Garda Thomas Dowling** (29) from Fanore, county Clare, ambushed and shot dead at Craggagh, Fanore, in reprisal for enforcement of illicit distillation law.

1926 November 14 – **Sgt James Fitzsimmons** (23) from Belfast, shot dead during armed raid on Garda station at Hollyford, county Tipperary and **Garda Hugh Ward** (29) died two days later of wounds suffered in same attack.

1929 June 11 – **Garda Timothy O'Sullivan** (32) from Knock, county Clare, killed by booby-trap bomb at Tullycrine, county Clare.

1931 March 21 – **Superintendent John David Curtin** (28) from Tipperary town, ambushed and shot dead outside his home in Tipperary.

1940 January 4 – **Garda John Roche** (34) from county Limerick, died a day after he was shot arresting a wanted man at McCurtain Street, Cork.

1940 August 17 – **Sgt Patrick McKeown** (39) from Blackrock, county Dublin, died a day after being shot along with **Garda Richard Hyland** from county Kildare, who was shot dead in the same attempt to arrest a wanted man at Rathgar, Dublin.

1942 September 9 – **Sgt Denis O'Brien** (41) native of Dublin, ambushed and shot dead outside his home at Ballyboden, county Dublin.

1942 October 1 – **Garda Michael Walsh** (41) from Cavan town, shot dead in Ballyjamesduff, attempting to arrest wanted man.

1942 October 10 – **Garda George Mordant** (45) from Dublin, shot dead when attempting to arrest a wanted man at Donnycarney, Dublin.

1970 April 3 – **Garda Richard Christopher Fallon** (44), from county Roscommon, shot dead at Arran Quay, Dublin, attempting to arrest five bank raiders.

1972 June 8 – **Inspector Samuel Donegan** (61) from county Longford, based at Cavan town. Killed by roadside booby-trap bomb at Newtownbutler, county Fermanagh.

1975 September 9 – **Garda Michael Joseph Reynolds** (30), native of county Galway, shot dead while attempting to arrest two armed bank raiders at Raheny, Dublin.

1976 October 16 - **Garda Michael Augustine Clerkin** (24), from Monaghan town, county Laois, killed by booby-trap bomb, Garryhinch, Portarlington, county Laois.

1980 July 7 - **Garda John Francis Morley** (37) and **Garda Henry Gerrard Byrne** (29) both from Knock, county Mayo, fatally wounded in pursuit of armed bank robbers.

1980 October 13 – **Garda James (Seamus) Quaid** (42), from county Limerick, shot dead at Ballyconnick, county Wexford attempting to arrest wanted man.

1982 February 2 – **Garda Patrick Gerald Reynolds** (23) from Kilmactranny, Boyle, county Roscommon, shot dead during search for stolen property while based at Tallaght, Dublin.

1983 April 11 – **Sgt Patrick Christopher Noel McLoughlin** (42) from Mullingar town, shot dead when answering night call at his home in Dunboyne, county Meath.

1983 December 12 – **Recruit Garda Peter Garry Mary Sheehan** (23), from Monaghan town, shot dead during Garda/Army search for kidnappers at Ballinamore, county Leitrim.

1984 August 10 – **Garda Francis Benedict Mary Hand** (29), from county Roscommon, shot dead while escorting post office van, Drumree, county Meath.

1985 June 27 – **Sgt Patrick Joseph Aquinas Morrissey** (48) from county Cavan, shot dead pursuing two armed men after armed raid on labour exchange at Ardee, county Louth.

1995 May 18 – **Sgt Paul M Reid** (39) from Dublin, fatally injured while on UN duty in Sarajevo,

1996 June 7 – **Jeremiah Desmond McCabe** (52) from Ballylongford, county Kerry, shot dead on post office truck escort duty, Adare, county Limerick.

1999 July 21 – **Sgt Andrew Callinan** (36) from Thurles, county Tipperary, died from injuries while attempting to save life of arsonist in early hours of the morning.

Appendix 3

Although separated by a period of 12 years, the remarkable parallels between the killing of Detective Jerry McCabe and the murder of Detective Frank Hand in county Louth starkly contrast with the very different outcomes of the subsequent trials. The murderous 1984 post office raid in which Detective Hand was shot dead and his partner wounded, also totally invalidated any IRA arguments then or since that its volunteers were bound by army standing orders that strictly ruled out military action against the security forces of the Republic.

In Adare, two Gardaí on escort duty with a post office truck came under fire, as a result of which one died and the second was wounded.

On a post office cash delivery run to Drumree in county Louth on 10 August 1984, the Garda duo in the escort car came under fire. One was killed, the other wounded.

In the case of Adare, four men went on trial at the Special Criminal Court on charges of capital murder in January-February 1999. The four pleaded 'not guilty'.

In the Drumree case, four men faced charges of capital murder before the Special Criminal Court in February-March 1985. All four entered 'not guilty' pleas.

In the Adare case, 'trial within a trial' proceedings were conducted to establish if certain statements made to Gardaí were admissible in evidence. A number of days of legal disputation had taken place over the admissibility of statements from a fifth man who was on trial on lesser charges.

In the Drumree case, 'trial within a trial' proceedings were conducted also to establish if statements presented in evidence by Gardaí would be admitted into evidence. In that case the four charged with capital murder gave evidence that they were not in Drumree on the day of the shooting and their stories were corroborated by the wives of three of the men in the dock.

In the Adare case, no evidence was presented to indicate who had fired the shots that killed Detective McCabe and the weapon involved had not been traced.

In the Drumree case, it was accepted by the court that the gunman who had fired the killer shots was not among the four on trial for capital murder. However, weapons had been found along with the cash from the post office raid five days after the crime.

In the Adare case, the judges of the Special Criminal Court were eventually not required to rule on the admissibility of the disputed statements when the State prosecution came to an agreement with the legal team for the defence.

In the Drumree case, the Special Criminal Court judges, with the Chief Justice, Mr Justice Liam Hamilton presiding, ruled that the statements provided by the Gardaí were admissible as evidence and rejected the defence case that in the questioning of the four, the interrogation had been excessive and threats and assaults had been involved.

In the Adare case, the State prosecution accepted pleas of guilty to manslaughter from the four before the court on capital murder charges and sentences of up to 14 years in prison were imposed.

In the Drumree case, three who had pleaded not guilty to the charges were found guilty of capital murder and sentenced to death, with the death penalty later commuted to 40 years in prison. A fourth man, who was said in evidence to have provided vehicles for the IRA, was convicted of murdering Garda Hand. The court held that in the case of the fourth man, the necessary intent to kill a Garda had not been proven by the prosecution, and handed down a sentence of life imprisonment. All four were released from prison in December 1998 under the early release provisions of the Good Friday Agreement having served 12 years in prison.

Chilling evidence was presented to the trial of the four involved in the capital murder of 27 year old Detective Hand just a week after his return from his honeymoon and marriage to a fellow detective.

Special Branch Detective, Michael Dowd, who was the passenger in the escort car driven by Detective Hand and the post office van driver, James Joseph Bell, gave evidence of orders to shoot being given when they were pushed prone onto the ground around the delivery van where Detective Hand lay dying.

Detective Dowd described in his evidence to the court how two armed men came running out of a gateway beside the Drumree post office where the Garda escort car and delivery van had pulled up. He told how one of the masked men armed with a handgun opened fire at the rear of the car and a second, holding a sub-machine gun, opened fire on the car and then went to the front of the Garda car and fired through the windscreen.

In the statements that were admitted into evidence by the judges, the court heard that those involved in the robbery had been told that if armed Gardaí were protecting the cash in transit, they would be 'dealt with'. Those involved in moving the bags of cash from the delivery van were told in pre-raid instructions that men 'who know what to do' were involved in the operation in the event of the Gardaí going for their guns. The evidence to the court was that two gunmen opened fire on the car before either of the detectives could shoot and before the driver, Detective Hand, went for his sidearm.

The court heard how Detective Dowd dropped the sub-machine gun from his lap when the Garda car came under fire. Evidence was given that, based on the wounds from which he died, Detective Hand had been shot in cross-fire while in a a crouched position as he attempted to get out of the car.

From Detective Dowd, the court heard that when he was grappling with the man who pulled him from the Garda car and was trying to push him to the ground, a figure giving orders shouted, 'Shoot him; fucking shoot him!' Evidence was also given by the survivors that the man giving orders had also instructed when the gang was making the getaway, 'If they move, shoot them.'